The Very Best
Home Improvement Guide
& Document Organizer

Alex A. Lluch

Author of Over 2 Million Books Sold!

WS Publishing Group
San Diego, California

The Very Best
HOME IMPROVEMENT GUIDE
& Document Organizer

By Alex A. Lluch

Published by WS Publishing Group
San Diego, California 92119
Copyright © 2007 by WS Publishing Group

Designed by WS Publishing Group:
David Defenbaugh and Sarah Jang

Photo Credit:
© Bill Reitzel/Photodisc Red/Getty Images

For Inquiries:
Logon to www.WSPublishingGroup.com
E-mail info@WSPublishingGroup.com

ISBN 13: 978-1-887169-78-3

Printed in China

place photo
of home here

The Home of:

_____

Address:

_____

_____

_____

"It takes hands to build a house, but only hearts can build a home."

~Author Unknown

TABLE OF CONTENTS

TABLE OF CONTENTS

PART 3: FILE FOLDERS

INTRODUCTION

The Very Best Home Improvement Guide & Document Organizer is an invaluable tool for keeping remodeling projects running smoothly, on time and on budget. It's fun to dream up new ideas for the home and make it everything you ever wanted. Now is the time to think about remodeling bathrooms, kitchens, room additions—whatever you desire. This is your home and your vision. It's OK if you're not sure where to begin or what to do; that's why *The Very Best Home Improvement Guide & Document Organizer* is here. You'll learn the entire process for making home improvements and how to bring a dream idea into reality.

Getting a new bathroom or kitchen, or making a room addition doesn't happen overnight and without a good deal of thought and planning. Whether your home improvement project is big or small, it all involves a number of steps and sub-projects. In this book, you'll learn just what those steps are and how to get through a myriad of details from deciding on the type of tiling in a bathroom or the cabinetry in the kitchen, to hiring designers.

Everything has its place and order, from setting a budget and prioritizing which areas to remodel first, to finding contractors, collecting bids and obtaining financing. It's easy to forget things as obvious as choosing a faucet in the bathroom, or skip an important step like funding the remodel, if you don't organize each detail. This is why *The Very Best Home Improvement Guide & Document Organizer* comes in handy. It will manage each step and keep you on track throughout the entire home improvement project.

Remodeling is rewarding when it's managed well. And you can do it! It's easy when you stick to a sensible and flexible plan. Projects that are organized free up your time so that you can stay focused on the end result: creating a more beautified home. There's nothing like seeing plans materialize before your eyes.

Along the way, you'll accumulate a ton of information, including design layouts, bids, contractor phone numbers, material quotes and so much more. Keeping your information all in one place prevents you from losing things and hunting for items at the last minute when you need them the most! This is why we have created *The Very Best Home Improvement Guide & Document Organizer.*

Our book is designed to make the home improvement process easy. Each chapter covers a topic to help you move forward with your project one step at a time. You'll learn everything you need to know about the project "Before You Start," and move right along in the process to "Personal Style," "Getting a Permit" and "Establishing a Budget." From there you'll encounter the comprehensive guides, "Financing Home Improvement," "Designers, Architects, and Contractors," and "Hiring a Contractor" and the importance of "Writing up a Contract" to "Minimizing Change Orders." Of course, you'll also learn the all-important essentials, "What to Do When Something Goes Wrong," "Design and Decorating Tips," and "What to Do When Partners Don't Agree."

We recommend that you read our book, *The Very Best Home Improvement Guide & Document Organizer,* before you begin any remodeling project and that you keep it handy.

On the other side of the book, you will find an accordion file where you can store design ideas, samples, product brochures, photographs, contracts, warranties, vendor and contact names, etc.

This accordion file includes the following categorized pockets:

- Paint
- Flooring
- Windows & Doors
- Cabinetry & Hard Surfaces
- Tubs, Toilets, Sinks

- Lighting & Lamps
- Appliances
- Electronics
- Exteriors
- Miscellaneous

These pockets will help you organize each aspect of your project by providing you with a single place to store each item. When you need to refer to a flooring photograph or the fine print of a contract, or locate the phone number of that helpful lighting consultant, you will be able to easily find it in its proper place. Use these handy pockets instead of laying essential paperwork and samples on a desk, stuffing them in a drawer or shoving them into the proverbial shoebox. Gather paint sample cards to your heart's delight. The pocket can hold them. Can't decide among the myriad of newfangled kitchen appliances, some of which you're not even sure what they do or if you need them? Go ahead and collect the brochures. You can decide later if you need that bread warmer, double oven or pot filler spigot installed over the stove.

"Home is where the house is."

~Child Age 6

BEFORE YOU START

Can you picture a kitchen that's a chef's delight or a bathroom with a home spa? Sure you can. This is the easiest part of any home improvement project. Let your imagination run wild. It's all part of the fun. This is your time to get as creative as any designer you've ever watched on a television home improvement show.

Before you begin this journey, think about all the projects you want to do and why. Ask yourself a few questions: Does your kitchen or bath need to be renovated? Is your current living space too small and cramped? Do you need an extra bedroom for another child on the way? Are you looking to add personal touches that reflect your unique style or make your space more functional? Would you like to have more outdoor living like a redwood deck, built-in barbecue or hot tub? Do you want to re-landscape the front of the house or change the color scheme of your living room?

After you've made a wish list of projects, ask yourself these realistic questions: Why do you want to renovate? Does it make financial sense? What is your budget? What is the desired time frame? How much work are you willing and able to do?

Now, prioritize your projects in order of importance and decide which projects you can afford. Consider how many years you plan to live in your house. The longer you are planning to stay in your house, the more it makes sense to improve your house to accommodate your needs.

If you are planning to sell your house in the near future, you may not want to spend too much money improving it. But keep in mind that cutting corners on a remodel could hurt more than help the sale potential of your home. People looking for a home can quickly spot inexpensive carpeting, bottom-of-the-line appliances and shoddy paint jobs. Also, prospective buyers may not want to pay for home design bonuses you added.

Future buyers visiting your house may not appreciate the time and energy it took you to find that perfect shade of red paint for your bedroom walls and the matching velour drapes, especially if they prefer white or muted colors. Think about what is important to a home buyer. Can you remember what features first attracted your interest in your home? What did you love about the house that compelled you to make an offer? Before you start planning upgrades with the intent of selling, consider this list of home improvement projects that buyers are likely to value:

- Updating the kitchen
- Adding or remodeling a bath
- Adding a room and increasing square footage
- Landscaping

Even if you are remodeling and plan to stay in your house for many years, resist the urge to go overboard. Someday you may sell the home. The rule of thumb in residential real estate sales is that your home should not be the most expensive house on the block. Any realtor will tell you such a home is more difficult to sell.

Find out home values in the area and try to keep your improvements in line with the neighborhood. Aim to keep your home's value at no more than 15-20% above the average. If your house is the only home on the block that has not been renovated and you've been in it a long time, or you bought it inexpensively because it was a "fixer-upper," chances are you will have plenty of financial room for improvements.

Unless you've recently moved into the home and prices haven't budged, you probably don't know the current value of your home. You can get an idea of the value of your house by calling a local real estate agent. Or pay for a professional appraisal of your house. Once you have a good idea of its value, add what you paid for your home, plus the estimated cost of your home improvement project. If your total comes to more than 20% above the average price of the homes in your neighborhood, you may want to rethink your project.

"A hard beginning maketh a good ending."

~John Heywood

PERSONAL STYLE

Next, think about what style you like. Does your taste lean more toward traditional, contemporary, country, Asian, southwestern or cottage? If you don't know your style, review our chapter on "Design and Decorating Tips." Search the Internet, flip through home decor magazines and browse through design books until you find a style that suits you best. Visit home shows, home improvement stores and designer showrooms in your area. Pay attention to style, functionality and whether it will work with your family's lifestyle, particularly if you have young children. It's important to have a very clear idea about what you like and what will work with your lifestyle. This will help you focus your design search.

When you find a style you like at a store or showroom, it's okay to incorporate that same look and feel into your home. It's why showrooms, magazines, design books, home shows and everyone else in the industry provide examples to consumers. They want homeowners to admire their style and buy their products. Consider it a marketing tactic that makes your life a bit easier. Just think how easy it would be to show your designer or contractor a magazine photograph of your dream kitchen, and say, "build me this."

While you're out looking at designer showrooms, be sure to collect brochures and samples of what you want to include in your project. Architects, designers and contractors rely on visuals. They need to see what you have in mind. Vague concepts about a design could be a huge source of frustration if the design team interprets things the wrong way.

Imagine your frustration when you expect an old-fashioned claw-foot tub, a freestanding Victorian sink with faucet, wainscoting, crown molding and period-appropriate cabinetry and lighting, and you wind up with a contemporary look. You need to be as specific and direct as you can be. Remember, if you want to make your life easier, then show the designers what you want. It's your best chance of having it delivered the way you want.

Consider every aspect of your project and what it entails. For example, if you're pursuing a kitchen remodel, collect samples and brochures of paint, wallpaper, flooring, cabinetry, appliances, lighting, countertops, backsplashes, sinks, plumbing fixtures, vents and windows. Unless money is absolutely no object, aim for items in the mid-range. You can always scale up, but it's harder to scale down when you set your heart on a specific product that throws your budget off course. Store your samples in the pockets in the back of this book.

Get to know everything you can about your choices. What do they look like when installed? What kind of maintenance do they require? How do they fare over time? What kinds of warranties are included? Try to see the products in real home situations.

If a stone company tells you they just installed a patio with the very stone you admire, ask them to make arrangements for you to visit the home. It's important for you to see how the stone looks displayed over a large area. What's appealing in a showroom display case may appear quite different on-site. You won't know unless you take the extra step. It's better to know ahead of time rather than after you've gone through the expense of purchasing materials and arranging for contractors to begin installation.

Familiarize yourself with the cost of the product from start to finish, even if you are working with an architect or designer. Know the market value and whether you are getting a fair deal or not. The cost of your project should include: professional fees, material, installation, labor and maintenance. Also, consider the durability and warranty of your materials.

"There is nothing like staying at home for real comfort."
~Jane Austen

GETTING A PERMIT

Depending on where you live, a home improvement project may require a permit. Therefore before you go too far, you should call your city building department and inquire if there are any special considerations you need to know about before embarking on your project. Every city has its own set of regulations. Even cities within the same county have different regulations.

For example, if you live in a historical neighborhood you may be restricted on what alterations can be made. You might not be able to paint the outside of your home that perfect shade of yellow rose if historical precedence requires you to paint it in a certain palette. There may be homeowner association restrictions or CC&Rs (covenants, conditions and restrictions) on the property. Your home may sit near sensitive wetlands, in which case there could be environmental restrictions. For home additions, there could be setback limits or height restrictions. You could also face zoning issues, depending on the complexity of what you want to do.

It's smart to talk to your local building department folks early in the process to find out about any restrictions that may apply. We are not talking about something as simple as changing the paint color in a room, wallpapering or upgrading furniture. But anything that will change a room's function usually requires a permit, such as: turning a bedroom into a bathroom; modifying a home's structure; adding a second story; or changing the electrical, plumbing or ventilation systems.

Be sure to ask your building department what type of permits you would need for your type of project, how far in advance you need to apply for them, and the costs of the permits. Not taking these various permits or regulations into consideration could be a big mistake.

NOTES:

_____

_____

_____

_____

_____

_____

_____

_____

_____

_____

_____

_____

_____

_____

_____

_____

_____

_____

_____

_____

_____

_____

_____

_____

_____

_____

_____

_____

"He is happiest, be he king or peasant, who finds peace in his home."

~Johann Wolfgang von Goethe

ESTABLISHING A BUDGET

Before you get too far into your plans, you need to have a heart-to-heart with your finances to figure out how much you can afford to spend on your project. No matter what your project is, it is very important that you have an idea about what you can afford or are willing to finance. Also, factor in enough cash reserves in case the project goes over time and budget. You don't have to hire anyone to get an idea about how much your project should cost. Ask friends, coworkers, family, and neighbors who recently remodeled what their costs ran. Though not everyone will share that information with you, there's no harm in asking. Some people love to tell their remodeling sagas. For many, it's a rite of homeowner passage.

You can also call an architect or interior designer, if you plan to use one, and ask for a preliminary estimate. If you don't plan to use a design professional but intend to go solo with a contractor, start calling contractors now to come look at your project and give you a general estimate. Tell them you want to get an idea about what your project might cost. Experienced contractors should be able to eyeball your project and give you an approximate cost range.

Consider the resources at your local home improvement store. Many now have kitchen or bathroom remodeling centers with advanced technology available to assist you in room layouts, color matches and all sorts of home improvement features. First, get familiar with their kitchen cabinets, appliances, plumbing hardware, surfaces, paint, and everything else you will need for your project.

When you have an idea about what you think you would like, sit down with one of their design professionals who can create a design template for you. Tell the designer which products you want to use. Within moments you will see how your project will look. You'll see if the cabinets are too modern for your tastes. Pick a different style and watch the change appear before your eyes. Keep adjusting until you come up with the design of your dreams. The designer will give you a quote on the project if you purchase it through their store. In this case, you have two options: 1) Pay for both the material and the installation from the store. This will very quickly give you an idea about how much your project will cost if you use their material and contractors. 2) The second option is to order the materials from the store and shop for your own contractor to do the installation. Since you will know the cost of materials, you can easily compare which options work best for you.

NOTES:

_____

_____

_____

_____

_____

_____

_____

_____

_____

_____

_____

_____

_____

_____

_____

_____

_____

_____

_____

_____

_____

_____

"Rome was not built in one day."

~John Heywood

FINANCING YOUR HOME IMPROVEMENT

There are many ways to finance home improvement projects. It all depends on your individual circumstances and financial needs. Whether it's by personal credit card, construction loan, home equity loan, or line of credit, there are numerous funding methods available to fit just about everyone's needs.

Consider these financing options and see which one works the best for you:

CREDIT CARDS

Some people choose to finance their home improvement projects on a personal credit card. However, unless you have a very low interest rate, the interest charges could keep you from paying off the balance for years, especially if costs run over time and budget. Only consider the credit card route if you can pay off the card quickly. Otherwise this project could end up costing you much more than you intended.

CONSTRUCTION LOANS

This type of loan is typically used for new home construction, not remodels. There are some creative construction/home improvement loans being offered, so they are worth researching at your local financial institutions. New homeowners usually take out this kind of loan to build the home, then either convert it to a conventional loan upon completion or take out a two-step construction-to-perm loan that automatically rolls into a conventional loan upon termination of construction. In general, short-term construction loans are fairly easy to obtain, but the interest rates are higher, so conversion at the close is imperative. Shop around. Some banks offer a 12-month home improvement construction loan that converts to a one-, three- or five-year adjustable rate mortgage at the completion of the project.

HOME EQUITY LOANS AND LINES OF CREDIT

A second mortgage, otherwise known as a home equity loan, is offered at either a fixed or adjustable rate. Either way, the rates are reasonable and the interest payments are tax deductible. A home equity line of credit is similar to a home equity loan except that you take out the funds as you need them, instead of a lump sum as occurs with a home equity loan. Both the regular home equity loan and the line of credit are made against the equity of your house. Typically, your bank will let you borrow up to 80% of your home's appraised value minus your first mortgage balance. For example, if your home is appraised at $500,000 and your first mortgage balance is $300,000, you could borrow $100,000. Another way of looking at this is to borrow 80% of $500,000 minus the first mortgage of $300,000.

How do you choose between a home equity loan or home equity line of credit?

A home equity line of credit makes more sense if you are financing a large home improvement project. It is easier to pay off a larger loan over a longer term. The monthly payments are a little easier to manage.

With the home equity loan, the bank issues the check in full, and you begin paying interest on the full amount right away, regardless of when you use it. If there are construction delays, you pay interest despite what's going on at the job site. This type of loan is fully amortized, secured by a mortgage or deed of trust in the second position on the title of your home.

If you intend to borrow somewhat small, fluctuating amounts and intend to quickly pay back the principal, a home equity line of credit can cost you less than a home equity loan. A home equity line of credit is usually based on a variable rate. Also, with a home equity line of credit, once the bank approves you for a specific amount, you can take out the cash on an as-needed basis without incurring more paperwork. This method allows you to pay your home improvement bills as you go along, but you're only responsible for the interest on what you've borrowed so far.

Another benefit to the home equity line of credit is that in the end, you only pay interest on the money you have actually borrowed. If you qualified for an $80,000 line of credit, but ended up using only $55,000, you only have to pay principle and interest on the $55,000 not the whole sum. If you had taken out a home equity loan, you would be responsible for principle and interest on the whole amount.

REFINANCING YOUR HOME

This type of loan requires you to pay off your old home mortgage loan and take out a new mortgage on your house. This type of financing makes sense if you can save at least two points on your current interest rate and have a rock-solid credit history, a steady job, and some equity built up in your home.

If you don't plan to stay long in your house, you might opt for a no-cost/no-point loan. These loans are a great bargain if you don't plan on being there for a long time (no more than two years). Although the interest rates are higher, you will save up-front by not paying the costs and points. Plus, you won't be in the home long enough to be burdened with the higher interest rate. The rule of thumb is that if you're "flipping" your house, keep closing costs and points low or eliminate them entirely. If you plan to stay in your house at least four or five years, it makes sense to pay closing costs and points to get a lower interest rate. In the long run, the lower interest rate will save you money. Make sure you understand points: they are up-front mortgage interest fees paid on a loan to reduce the initial interest rate.

When a broker or lender pays all the closing costs on a loan, it is commonly referred to as a "no closing cost" loan, sometimes referred to as a no-cost/no-point loan. These closing costs occur at one time and include the appraisal, title and escrow, lender, credit report, administrative, origination, underwriting, wire transfer, mortgage broker, points, document preparation, tax service and flood certification. Closing costs exclude recurring items like interest, insurance and property taxes.

OTHER LOANS

Some people prefer to take out a personal loan, also called an unsecured or signature loan, because it is not secured to collateral, i.e. the home or possessions. Unsecured loans are based on income and past credit history. Interest rates run higher on these kinds of loans, and the interest cannot be deducted from taxes. With a steady job, you'll have a good chance of obtaining this kind of loan.

If you have a blemished credit report and cannot apply for a conventional loan, or you want the money quickly and have the means to pay it off in the short term, then consider an unsecured loan. The key with this kind of loan is to pay it off sooner, rather than later. Otherwise the high interest rate and the inability to deduct it from a tax return could make the home improvement project too expensive.

Another option is that if you participate in a 401(k) or 403(b) plan at work, you might be able to obtain a short-term loan from your account. Ask your human resources benefits officer if this is possible and ask your accountant what the tax implications will be.

A creative, albeit unconventional option is to borrow against your life insurance policy. Ask your insurance agent if your policy allows this and get the details for this type of loan.

If you're ready to go loan shopping, check with your personal bank and a few competing financial institutions to find out about their loan programs, competitive rates and financing terms. Don't forget to use the Internet, where you can find a number of very reputable companies who offer competitive loans online.

Once you find the type of loan you want, fill out an application and establish how much you can borrow. The $100,000 dream kitchen might not be doable. On the other hand, you might discover you qualify for more than you thought. Besides interest rate, be sure to ask about the length of the loan, early payoff and penalties, what fees apply, balloon payments, fixed or adjustable interest rates, and if they offer any special deals such as an introductory rate or waived fees. Ask the same questions at all the financial institutions you visit so you can compare apples to apples.

"Home, the spot of earth supremely blest, a dearer, sweeter spot than all the rest."
~Robert Montgomery

DESIGNERS, ARCHITECTS AND CONTRACTORS

You might be the type of person who can visualize every aspect of the home remodel design, can roll with the punches when problems arise and don't mind being on-site every step of the way. Most people lack such time and knowledge and find that projects like this are best left to the pros. You can choose designers, architects and contractors to handle your remodel. It all depends on your project needs and circumstances. Many of these professionals offer cost-saving ideas that you as an outsider might be unaware of. To get an idea about which design professional makes the most sense for your project, review the following overview of each of their specialties.

DESIGNERS

Getting the design of your dream—yes it's possible. If you have a natural flare for knowing just what looks right with what, or are on a tight budget, then you might want to forgo the expense of going with a designer. Otherwise, consider working with a designer; it can be quite spectacular to have the décor match the space and dynamics of a room. The goal of interior design is to optimize and harmonize the use of space on the inside of the house. This includes anything from a kitchen, bath or family room, to a master bedroom. Occasionally interior designers also work on outdoor projects such as patios or porches.

Several factors come into play when an interior designer presents a solution, including: the size of the room, how the space will be used, personal tastes and preferences, and the building construction. Practical considerations like accessibility, health issues, lighting, acoustics, seating and places to store and display items are also factored into the design.

If you decide to use an interior designer, you should still do your homework by collecting samples and brochures. The more visual information cues you can give your designer the better. It makes it easier for them to present a concept you'll love and one that reflects your style and goals for the room(s). To locate an interior designer, check the local chapter of the American Society of Interior Designers (ASID), www.asid.org.

ARCHITECTS

If your project involves major construction and requires that the addition blend into the current structure and landscape, it is advisable to consult with a residential architect. Architects are licensed professionals with the education, training and experience to manage and guide you through the entire design and construction process. They can help you define what to build, recommend various design options and make sure the structure adheres to building codes, zoning laws and permit requirements.

They not only prepare the design and blueprints for your home remodeling project, but also work with your contractor to ensure the project is implemented properly, resulting in a blended final effect. Architects also offer suggestions on materials and supervise construction. Granted, these professionals aren't cheap, but not using one in certain circumstances could cost you more in mistakes, time and expenses. To locate an architect, check with the American Institute of Architects (AIA), www.aia.org.

GENERAL/SPECIALIZED CONTRACTORS

General Contractors

A general contractor (GC) is a multi-tasker, organizer and a visionary of sorts. The contractor juggles multiple projects, anticipates what happens in what order and is prepared for the next step. This requires good foresight, thinking ahead and coordinating a dizzying number of details. The contractor orders materials and supplies to arrive in time for the start of each portion of the project, lines up subcontractors (tradespeople), sets their daily schedule, supervises their work and pays them. Plus, they often file for permits and arrange for building inspections on each part of the project. Without those city inspections, the project comes to a halt. If you've hired a designer or architect, the contractor has to interact with him or her too, plus consult with you on a daily basis and do it all with a smile, even when the building inspector just told your contractor that a new wall is off kilter and has to be torn down and rebuilt. To locate a general contractor, check with the Associated General Contractors of America (AGC), www.agc.org.

Kitchen and Bath Specialists

There are firms that specialize in certain types of projects such as kitchens and baths. Many of these firms provide both design and construction services. It's sort of one-stop shopping. These firms are definitely worth considering because they are very experienced in designing and building the specific type of project you want. Look for companies who employ designers with designations earned through specific education, training and experience. For kitchens, seek out a Certified Kitchen Designer (CKD); for bath remodels, look for a Certified Bath Designer (CBD), both of which have been licensed and certified by the National Kitchen and Bath Association (NKBA), www.nkba.org.

Landscaping Architects or Landscape Contractors
If you need help with a patio, porch or landscaping, consult with a landscape architect or landscape contractor. A landscape architect ensures your project's success by performing site analysis and feasibility studies to determine that the land or yard can accommodate the ideas and ground disruption. Their design plans account for soil water retention, storm water runoff, soil erosion, stability, and other soil conditions that could affect design. Like a landscape contractor, they recommend plants and trees that will work well in your region.

A landscape contractor offers a different array of services, including: design, installation and maintenance of your property. Many landscape firms employ landscape architects and designers who create the complete design and contractors who carry out the plans. Landscape contractors not only install plant material, but also install hardscapes such as: porches, patios, decks, retaining walls, gazebos and irrigation systems. To find a landscape contractor, go to the Professional Landcare Network (PLANET), www.landcarenetwork.org.

These days, sophisticated computer software helps you see what your completed landscape job will look like before anyone digs up the first shovelful of dirt. It used to be that landscape designers and contractors presented homeowners with 3-D images and drawings of design ideas. Unless you are a designer, these kinds of images can be hard to visualize. Now landscape contractors can take a digital photograph of your house and yard, and produce computer generated images of various designs. It's really exciting to be able to see the various design possibilities appear as if they are completed. Sketches are nice, 3-D is better, but these computer-generated photos are the most realistic. Ask your landscape architect or contractor if they use virtual landscaping programs.

Do you consider yourself an exceptional gardener and want to help design your outdoor space? You can invest in software that will help you build your design and see how it will look. If you don't like how a weeping willow dominates the corner, exchange it for an apple tree or a jacaranda. There are several programs for under $20 available in stores and online.

NOTES:

_____

_____

_____

_____

_____

_____

_____

_____

_____

_____

_____

_____

_____

_____

_____

_____

_____

_____

_____

_____

_____

_____

_____

_____

_____

"What is once well done is done forever."

~Henry David Thoreau

FINDING AND HIRING
A CONTRACTOR

If your project is something extremely simple like changing the faucets on your sinks, you can hire a licensed plumber or a good handyperson. The same goes for new built-in custom bookshelves ... call in a talented carpenter or woodworker. If you want to upgrade the air conditioning in your home, look for an air conditioning contractor. Need new flooring in your game room? Check out flooring contractors or visit a flooring showroom. Tired of your home's white walls and want to spruce it up with some color? Call a painting contractor. Perhaps you have a few simple "fix-it" projects that do not require great expertise or coordination with ancillary parts of your home. Many homeowners could do these types of repairs themselves, but if you're not particularly adept at home repair, or if you don't have the time, find yourself a skilled handyperson.

If you are ready for a major renovation such as a room addition or a second story, you may want to consider hiring a general contractor (GC). This chapter explains the process of hiring either a small contractor (painter or carpenter) or a large company's general contractor.

THE CONTRACTOR SEARCH

How do you find a contractor? Architects and designers are excellent sources for contractor recommendations. They work with reputable contractors every day. In fact, they base their reputations and livelihoods on these relationships and are not about to recommend someone who cannot complete the job with the highest level of satisfaction.

If you are not going to use a designer or architect, finding the right contractor who is a good fit for your project will take some legwork on your part. Begin by asking real estate agents, designers, neighbors, friends, coworkers, family members and your financial institution for the names of reputable contractors.

Banks that grant construction loans work with contractors in your area and know the reputable ones. Another way to get names is to call your local builders association for a list of their members, or contact the National Association of the Remodeling Industry, www.nari.org. NARI members are certified and come with more credibility than a state contracting license, which in some places is as easy to get as paying a fee and filling out paperwork. Other states like California go to great lengths to make sure those who receive a state contracting license are well-qualified.

If none of these avenues produces any viable names, you can stop by your local hardware or home improvement store and ask for recommendations, as well as check your local yellow pages or newspaper ads. This is the most risky way to go, because these names do not come with endorsements from people you know and trust. Another way to find names is to check your local city magazine, newspaper and websites for their "Best Of" lists. They often list remodeling contractors. If someone has won an award in this category, that's a good recommendation.

Is there a house in your neighborhood that has recently undergone a renovation? Stop by and ask the homeowner if they are pleased with their remodel and the whole experience. Ask if you can take a look at the completed project.

Be sure to ask the homeowner the following questions:

- Did the contractor stay on budget? If not, why? (It could be that the homeowners changed their minds mid-construction, and the contractor had to tear out a shower and start over.)

- How did the contractor handle adding on items and changing orders not included in the original budget? Determine if the change order charges sound reasonable or not.

- Did the contractor stay on-site to oversee the project? If not, did the contractor have someone to stand in when he or she wasn't there?

- What work did the contractor perform, and what is the quality of that work?

- Did the job site get cleaned up each day? Did the contractor try not to disrupt the rest of the home? Sometimes it isn't possible, but it's nice to know if the contractor makes an effort.

- How close did the construction and completion timetable come to the original time frame? If it didn't meet the specified time period, find out what influenced the delay.

- How many contractors presented bids on the job?

- Did the necessary building permits come through in a timely manner? Who obtained the permits: the homeowner or the contractor?

- How did the contractor schedule building inspections? Did it cause any problems in getting approvals? Did work have to be repeatedly redone?

- Did the homeowner sign a contract and examine the contractor's state license, insurance, and workers' compensation policy?

- What is it like to work with this contractor? Is the contractor a "take charge" kind of person or laid back and easygoing? Bear in mind that you and the contractor will be spending a lot of time together. If you choose someone whose personality style grates on you, your project can and will seem like the endless winter of discontent.

Once you gather the names of some reputable contractors, call and invite them to your home to see the space you want renovated. Request bids from at least three contractors. Sometimes contractors will tell you your project is too big or too small for their business. Hopefully this will happen on the phone before either of you invest considerable time in the process. If that's the case, don't try to argue or talk the person into your project. The contractor is telling you he or she is not interested. Accept their decision and continue with your search.

INTERVIEWING CONTRACTORS

One of the biggest goals of the first meeting is to get a feel for the person. Determine if you can work together and communicate. Establish whether you have chemistry and are compatible. This person doesn't have to be your soul mate, but you do have to be able to get along. Did the person arrive on time to meet with you? Is the person courteous and respectful? The ability to communicate is probably the most important characteristic a contractor can possess, aside from skill and expertise.

Here are a number of items you'll need to cover at this first meeting:

- Review the contractor's experience with this type of project. How many related projects has she or he done, and over what time frame?

- How many years has the contractor been in business?

- Does the contractor have a contractor's license in your state?

- How much liability insurance does the contractor carry? Don't forget to ask whether he or she carries a workers' compensation policy. If the contractor you ultimately hire does not have insurance, and this is the person you feel can best execute your job, make sure your own insurance will cover any potential accidents.

- Will the contractor acquire necessary permits, or will the architect get them? Can you save some money by getting them yourself? If you must acquire the permits, find out if the contractor will tell you when to file.

- How long does the contractor expect the project will take, and how much disruption will it cause your home? Will the job site be cleaned up every day?

- Discuss payment options. Find out if the contractor will allow you to make a down payment prior to the job, a second payment when the job is complete, and a final payment of 15% when you are satisfied that it has been completed to your specifications.

- Ask about the contractor's policy on project cancellation.

- When will work begin, and how long does the contractor estimate it will take?

- How much of the job will be subcontracted and to whom?

- Does the contractor hire the same subcontractors on a regular basis?

- Who will be on the job every day—the contractor or a foreman?

- Who will be the contractor during the job, and how regularly will you have access to that person?

- If the contractor offers to cut a significant percentage off the total price if you sign a contract right away, consider the interview over and do not hire him. This is a huge red flag! Legitimate contractors do not operate in this manner, but scam artists do. They are the same ones that go door to door telling you they are working in the neighborhood and have leftover materials and will cut you a deal if you hire them on the spot. They will cause you nothing but grief. Besides, you probably don't want someone like that in or around your house, especially without references, background checks or interviews.

- How does the contractor charge for change orders?

- Will the contractor guarantee his/her work?

• Give each contractor an exact copy of your plans/graph papers/sketches and specifications. Make the exact same request of each of the contractors so you will be able to compare apples to apples. Make sure you request that the bids detail every small aspect of the job from how much each of the subcontractors will be paid, to the cost for materials, colors and brands, to the cost of rental equipment, appliances, manufacturers and styles of cabinetry, change order charges, etc. Don't ask one to give you a quote for a kitchen with hardwood flooring and another to quote the same kitchen with vinyl flooring. If you can't decide, ask each contractor to quote on both types of flooring. Be accurate and fair. Find out how long it will take the contractors to prepare a written bid and when you can expect to hear from them.

Besides the bids, ask each contractor for the following items:

• At least three homeowner references of the most recent completed jobs, plus whatever project is underway. Beware if the contractor gives you a reference from a job finished several years ago. This could be a big red flag. Call these homeowners and ask if you can see the completed project. When you get to their home, ask the same set of questions listed on pages 28-29 for homeowners in your neighborhood.

• The contractor's state license; insurance certificate to verify current workers' compensation; general liability insurance and property damage; and personal liability in case of accidents.

• The contractor's permanent, local business location. Some very good contractors work out of their homes. That's fine as long as they have a good reputation with local banks, suppliers, subcontractors and building inspectors as well as the proper certification, licensing and insurance coverage.

• References for you to verify the contractor's business practices. You don't want to hire a contractor who doesn't pay his/her subcontractors or suppliers on time and can't manage his/her business. That's a surefire sign he/she might have trouble managing the complexities of your project.

Call the Better Business Bureau (BBB) to verify how long the company has been in business and whether there are any unsettled complaints against the contractor. If your BBB does not keep any complaint files or have any on a particular contractor, call your consumer affairs office or attorney general's office to find out if anyone has lodged a complaint or filed a lawsuit. Just because a homeowner has filed a complaint against a contractor is no reason to scratch this person off your list. For all you know, the contractor might have found him or herself working for Attila the Hun. Call the contractor and ask what happened. Give the contractor an opportunity to explain his or her side of the story. If the contractor was maligned, he or she will appreciate the opportunity to clarify the story. If the contractor reacts defensively or gets angry, that will tell you volumes. Then you can determine if you want to work with someone who behaves like that. Above all, take your time during your exploratory meetings and during your research to investigate the contractors you interview. Most problems occur when homeowners fail to research contractors before hiring them.

When you have finished checking out the contractors, ask them to give you written bids. These days it's easiest to do this via fax or email. Go over the bids and pick the two that best meet both your requirements and budget. Then ask these two contractors to come back and meet with you one last time to go over their bids in person. During your second meeting you may pick up on a personality trait you did not notice before. Or you may find that one of them simply stands out from the other.

After the final meetings, consider the bids along with what you have learned about each contractor. Bear in mind that you don't have to accept the lowest bid. In fact it may not be a good idea to accept the lowest. Be cautious of the particularly low bid or what seems like an inexpensive advertised price. This could be a red flag of someone who either doesn't know what he or she is doing, or is so strapped for cash the person is taking on a job to pay for a previous job also underbid.

"Many hands make light work."

~John Heywood

WRITING UP A CONTRACT

If you have a large and/or complex project, you may prefer to have an attorney review or write up the contract. There are also a number of very good pre-printed contracts available at home improvement stores and on the Internet. Take a look at the sample contract provided by the American Institute of Architects, www.aia.org.

Some contracts are more comprehensive and user-friendly than others. Whatever you decide, do not go forward without a signed contract. Should anything go wrong, if you don't have a contract, you'll be in a deep well of trouble.

Make sure your contract includes both general and specific items. General items encompass things like: names, addresses, phone numbers, license numbers, dates, job description, required materials, subcontractors, estimated length of construction, cancellation policies, warranties, etc.

Specific contract items include:

Financial terms of the contract: These need to be very clear and not the least bit ambiguous. The contract should include the complete price, payment schedule, cancellation policy and details about financing, particularly if it's a loan. You might need a clause that the contract will be null and void if you don't obtain the financing or cannot obtain financing at agreeable terms.

Down payment: Before the project begins you will need to make a down payment. Some contractors require 30%; others will take less. Negotiate this ahead of time and spell it out in the contract. Only the down payment is made ahead of time. After that, do not make payments for work until it has been completed to your satisfaction.

Material used: The contract should stipulate in detail all materials that will be used in the project. Include details such as: the grade or quality, quantity, size, weight, color and brand of all the materials to be used. Don't list just white paint, but the specific name and manufacturer of the paint you want. Otherwise the contractor can use any paint at their discretion. You may have wanted a specific paint that is easy to wash (for those "accidental" crayon drawings the munchkins in your house may add to your wall décor.) Unless it's spelled out, the contractor may opt to use a non-washable paint.

Warranties in writing: Read the warranties and make sure they cover what you are being told they will cover.

Change orders: Include a clause on how change orders will be handled. See the next chapter for advice on change orders.

Additional items:

• Mention that the contractor is responsible for cleanup at the end of the day, or specify which party will pay for cleanup.

• Request the contractor show up for work in person every day.

• Write an arbitration clause and attorney's fees clause for the prevailing party.

• Require the contractor to carry insurance and workers' compensation.

• Stipulate penalty for canceling the job.

• It's smart to include a clause about dispute settlement. If you and your contractor know going in that you will both make an effort to resolve disagreements rather than let them escalate, it sets a cordial tone for doing business. When and if an insurmountable difficulty arises, both of you know what avenues are at your disposal.

• Put everything in writing, including verbal assurances. Indicate in precise terms what the contractor will and will not do. Be very specific. For example, if you propose to perform some of the work yourself, include this in the contract.

• Do not sign a blank contract or even a partially blank contract. Even if it is a contract you paid an attorney to write, read every word before you sign on the dotted line. Sign the contract and make sure you get a copy after you and your contractor sign it. Keep it in a safe place.

• Remember that home improvement contracts typically specify three working days to cancel the contract should you get cold feet and change your mind. It's a federal law called the Right of Recision.

"He who never undertook anything never achieved anything."

~French Proverb

MINIMIZING CHANGE ORDERS

Let's state one well-known fact about home improvement up front. Change orders are an inevitable part of any home renovation project. They cannot be avoided. While you try to plan out every detail, when a project is underway, something will turn out differently than expected. Maybe the big picture window you envisioned is too large and casts too much afternoon sun into a room. Perhaps a lovely shade of ochre you picked out for your bedroom walls makes you feel a little queasy. Or the flooring subcontractor takes up your old tile and finds extensive termite damage to the subfloor. This may require that they rip out and replace the entire floor before they can proceed.

WHAT IS A CHANGE ORDER AND HOW CAN IT AFFECT THE PROJECT?

A change order alters an aspect of the project. It could be expanding the size of a room, widening or narrowing a door, adding a closet, moving a sink or buying a larger stove. Every change generates a new cost and extends the time frame.

Design professionals, contractors and subcontractors have to stop work, go back, change the plans and rearrange the work schedule. Sometimes this will mean acquiring a new permit, reordering and waiting for parts. It may impact other elements of the job, requiring adjustment to accommodate the change.

For example, moving the sink may require rearranging the entire kitchen layout. If construction has already begun when you make changes, you can count on increasing costs and time. When there's an overwhelming reason to modify something, it makes sense. Otherwise try to stick with the original plan. You will still encounter change orders, but they will be minimal, unless your house has some big surprises for you.

Change orders are often the greatest source of grief during home improvement. If changes are required mid-project, the contractor will often have to tear the project apart to start over, and this will likely impact other subsequent parts of the job. This may also mean the contractor will have to pay overtime to avoid further delays or pay the subcontractors two or three times more than what they had budgeted.

Some unscrupulous contractors will take advantage of the homeowner and charge whatever they want for change orders. However, most legitimate and honest contractors do not work this way. If you have done your homework and researched the contractor, chances are you will not encounter this type of situation. But you never know, so you need to take steps to protect yourself.

A good way to minimize the impact of change orders is to discuss them before any work begins. Discuss it when you interview potential contractors. Also bring it up at the bidding stage and make sure your contract includes a change order clause. Remember change orders can significantly increase the cost of your project. It often costs more to redo something after the project has started than to make changes before work has begun.

Your contract should specify that you have the right to make changes to the plan. The contract should state that when a change is going to be made, you and the contractor will negotiate the terms and details. Specify details about the change in an agreement that both you and your contractor will sign and attach to the contract. This "mini" agreement should spell out the proposed change, the price you and your contractor agree upon and an expected end date, if one can be determined.

You may want to specify in your contract clause that the contractor will limit his or her change order profit percentage to a predetermined amount agreed to beforehand. For example, you can agree to pay time and material plus a 20% profit for the contractor. Also stipulate the hourly fee for the contractor or his/her employees for each change order.

It's understood that the contractor needs to make a profit; just specify what is reasonable. It must be fair to everyone—the homeowner, the contractor and the subcontractors. If the change order is going to throw off your project's schedule and the successive jobs in your project, make sure the contractor puts that in writing so it is clear to everyone.

"Construction and home improvement projects operate on the 3/5 rule.
Most jobs end up taking three times the time and five times the money."
~Anonymous

WHEN SOMETHING GOES WRONG

Begin any type of home improvement project with your eyes wide open and your paperwork in place. Protect yourself so that just in case something does go wrong, you'll have avenues for relief.

The first and smartest thing you can do, as outlined in the chapter "Writing Up a Contract," is to ensure there is a clause in your contract about what you and your contractor will do in the event of a dispute. We don't mean minor things like not returning a phone call, but major issues such as putting in the wrong sink, installing tile instead of hardwood on your floor or a behavioral issue with one of the subcontractors.

Before you go looking for a lawyer, take a deep breath and look at your contract to review what you agreed upon in the event of a dispute. Hopefully your contract says both parties agree to pursue mediation, and if that avenue doesn't work, then arbitration.

TALK TO YOUR CONTRACTOR

The first step is to call your contractor. Explain the nature of the problem and ask for a quick resolution. Give your contractor the opportunity to explain his or her side of the story. If the problem is caused by a misinterpretation of the design plans, call your design professional and get them involved in a face-to-face discussion.

With a thorough contract you should be able to resolve issues like this in a prompt fashion. For example, if incorrect materials were used, you can point to the section in the contract where it describes the type of material to be installed. Your contractor will have to make good on the contract.

On the other hand, let's say that the contract simply says "white kitchen sink," and your contractor installed a basic white sink. However, you had envisioned a rustic, off-white farm-style sink. The contractor would not be at fault because this was not specified in the contract. In this instance, you will need to pay to have the wrong sink taken out, and possibly pay to adjust the counters and surrounding cabinetry to accommodate the sink you wanted. At that point you might want to rethink whether you could live with this "other" sink.

Before you call your contractor, take a good look at the agreement and think through the problem. Determine if this is a case of breach of contract, careless/inferior work, miscommunication or non-documentation. The source of the problem will determine who will pay to fix it.

Bottom line: Talk to your contractor. You picked this person because you connected with him, right? That was one of your great deciding factors in choosing this particular professional. Whatever you do, don't start making accusations or bullying to get what you want. Listen first. Then discuss what happened and try to negotiate a solution. Even if you know you are right, try to come up with a workable solution. Don't make it about ego. Rather, be ready to compromise in order to move ahead with your project.

MEDIATION

Let's say you talked to your contractor and the two of you can only agree that you disagree. What do you do next?

If your contract called for bringing in a mediator to resolve disputes, now is the time to do that. There are a number of places to go for mediation help. Refer to the Alternative Dispute Resolution (ADR) Act for more information. Congress passed this act to provide less expensive and less contentious ways to resolve disputes than traditional contract litigation.

How do you find a mediator? If you did not specify a mediator in your contract, start with your local Better Business Bureau. If your contractor is a member, the BBB can provide conciliation, mediation, or arbitration services. Another place to find ADR services is your city or county courthouse.

You can also check with the American Arbitration Association, www.adr.org, founded in 1926. They offer the gamut of resolution services such as: mediation, arbitration, and other out-of-court settlement techniques. The organization operates 34 offices in the United States and Europe. Not only do they provide a forum for hearing disputes and applying case tested rules and procedures, but you can also search for a mediator in your area through them.

One thing you should be aware of if you go the mediation route is that a mediator does not settle the dispute. The parties settle the dispute when they come to the realization that it is in their best interests to do so. This usually happens when both sides realize it's costing both of them a lot of time, money and aggravation.

A mediator's job is to keep both parties talking and discussing solutions. Mediators will listen to each party's argument and point out strengths and weaknesses of the case. Think of it as assisted negotiation with a referee orchestrating communication between the two sides. Mediators often encourage one party to paraphrase the other party's argument to ensure both parties are actively listening to each other.

Even though a compromise is required (each side must give something in order to reach a consensus), mediation is still an empowering process. Mediation is conducive to helping both parties feel they are in control of their own outcome—unlike arbitration or court. When the two sides come to an agreement, they sign a legally binding document recording their understanding.

ARBITRATION

Arbitration is the next level up for dispute resolution before filing a lawsuit. An independent third party makes a mostly private binding judgment. There are three forms of arbitration: commercial, consumer and employee/labor. Yours would be consumer.

An arbitration hearing can involve a single arbitrator or a tribunal, which can be comprised of several arbitrators. When you and your contractor hire an arbitrator or tribunal, you allow them to judge the dispute. Like mediation, arbitration is an alternative to going to court. Keep in mind that arbitration can sometimes be just as expensive as going to trial if the arbitrator charges a high hourly rate and the arbitration goes on an inordinate amount of time. It can also be as stressful as a regular trial.

Arbitrators and tribunal members are usually appointed by one of several ways:

• You and the contractor decide on an arbitrator together. It is wise to designate an arbitrator in your contract so you don't have to deal with this decision after things get dicey. After all, if you can't agree on how to resolve the issue, it will likely be just as difficult to agree on an arbitrator.

• Another way is for each of you to appoint your own arbitrator. Your two arbitrators appoint a third, creating a tribunal.

• If this doesn't work, an external party, such as an arbitration association or a court, will appoint an arbitrator for you.

State and federal laws govern arbitration. Most states have adopted the Uniform Arbitration Act; however, some states follow their own particular arbitration rules. Within the particular state, provisions provide a basic model and procedures for attaining and confirming an arbitrator's award. This is the document that explains the arbitrator's decision. There is also a procedure that will give the award some "teeth"—the muscle that enforces the judgment, just as if you went to trial and a judge made the decision.

LITIGATION

Hopefully, this has given you some avenues to consider instead of litigating your case. If none of these alternatives seem plausible and you are intent on filing a lawsuit, then go in with your eyes wide open.

Lawsuits can be the more expensive way to go. Unless you suffered huge damages and it is absolutely obvious there was a breach of contract, inferior work was performed or you were deceived, you may end up losing more than you gain. And if you lose, you may have to pay your contractor's attorney's fees as well as your own. These details can best be determined by a lawyer.

Seek out a lawyer who specializes in construction law. Ask any lawyers you know for referrals. If you secured a loan, ask your financial institution for names of construction lawyers. Finally, you can always check with your local bar association for referrals. Interview a couple of attorneys until you find someone compatible with your needs.

"Law of the Workshop: Any tool, when dropped,
will roll to the least accessible corner."

~Anonymous

DESIGN AND DECORATING TIPS

Perhaps the most important rule to keep in mind when thinking about decorating and design is that there are no hard-and-fast rules. Years ago, there were set notions about what you should do in a home. Not anymore.

Just because a renowned designer says that all white rooms or earth tones are in vogue is not a reason for you to follow suit, particularly if you love deep ocean colors. You are the one who has to live in your home, not the designer. It used to be that you couldn't mix patterns and more than a couple of colors in a room. Visit any design showroom and you will see this has changed.

Keep in mind that trends fade fast. Most cycle out after three years. So if you decide to follow the latest trend, your house may look dated in a few short years. To prevent this scenario, try to avoid trends and stick with timeless designs and decor.

Depending on what part of the country you call home, you may want to pursue a regional look. For example, on the east coast, Cape Cod is a time-honored architectural style; while in New Mexico, parts of Arizona and Colorado, many homes feature southwestern architecture and interior decor.

Maybe you don't have a clue what style you like. If that's the case, spend some time browsing through design, architecture and decorating magazines and websites. Watch home renovation and decorating shows on television. Stop in designer showrooms and furniture stores. Observe the different styles and get a sense for what feels comfortable to you. Become familiar with them; find what works best for your environment, family and frame of mind.

POPULAR DESIGN AND DECORATING STYLES

African/Safari
This style attempts to recreate the look of the African plains. Furniture and coverings emulate animal prints and African textiles. Hard surfaces flow with safari desert tones highlighted with sapphire, vermilion, pumpkin orange and mahogany. Tribal baskets, ewe cloth, and Ashanti Adinkra symbols from Ghana add authenticity. Aboriginal African art hangs on walls.

Asian

Asian ambience is considered both exotic and soothing to the soul. Chinese and Japanese designs relay tranquility. Natural elements of wood, water and plant material mark the decor. Bamboo and grass cloth elements dominate Asian furniture.

Chinese furnishings tend to be more upright and formal than Japanese. Chinese style also follows a balanced or yin and yang, symmetrical arrangement of room layout. The positioning of objects in a mindful way to increase flow and harmony is an ancient Chinese art called feng shui. Red prevails; it is considered good luck. Chinese furnishings come highly styled, often with lacquer finishes, hand-painted designs, and statues of animals and mythical creatures.

In Japanese homes, rice-paper lanterns cast soft, tranquil lighting. Bedrooms feature shoji screens, tatami mats and futons for sleeping. Unlike Chinese furnishings, the furniture features clean, plain lines in muted colors devoid of adornment. The furniture sits low to the ground. Japanese style stresses horizontal rather than vertical lines.

Arts and Crafts

This stylistic movement embraces craftsmanship and uncomplicated lines. Once considered radical, Arts and Crafts décor now emulates taste and tradition. Fabrics and wallpapers often imitate Gothic, floral and Japanese designs. Furniture tends to be block-shaped and is usually made of oak. Colors are generally warm—crimson, tawny beige, grassy green and subdued cerulean blue. Neutral tones such as ivory and gray stone are also common. Materials range from dark leathers, to rich fabrics like cotton chintzes, linens, wools and silks. These homes feature wooden floors covered with muted Oriental or flat-woven rugs in nature-oriented patterns. Stone flagging and earth-colored ceramic tiles embellish entryways and fireplaces.

Recognizable Arts and Crafts furniture include Gustav Stickley's Mission pieces. Lighting is both tasteful and useful, as evidenced by Louis Comfort Tiffany's intricate stained-glass lamps and Dick Van Erp's hammered copper lamps.

Coastal

Soothing and easy on the eyes and spirit, coastal colors create a casual ambience. Pastel colors prevail, but not in a feminine way. Rooms are tranquil with pale blue, light teal, bleached white, sea green, and buff. Accents range from silver metals and bleached woods like bamboo to water-washed finishes on furniture and accessories. Beach themes reign—speckled with sailboats, shells, birds, dolphins and sea horses. More nautically oriented rooms may incorporate ropes sporting knots, lifesavers, a boat's wooden steering wheel, a diver's helmet, fishing nets and sculptures of lighthouses.

Cottage Style

The Cottage look often evolves from garage sales, flea markets, or family hand-me-downs. Nothing really matches, yet the entire effect is cozy, charming and welcoming. Pieces look seasoned with signs of cherished wear and gentle aging. Imperfection is the key to this look. Anything new can and should be made to look rustic. Throw rugs and area rugs cover bare floors. Window coverings look light and almost ethereal. Mix up fabrics and prints but concentrate on soft, airy colors with a harmonizing theme. Bead boarding adds a nice accent. For a garden look, choose floral prints with rose, lilac and green. For a more natural look, use soft baby blue, off-white and sandy beige.

English Country

Defined as relaxed and comfortable, English Country is a variation on traditional English period styles. Colors tend to be vivid and garden-like. Rugs are frequently fussy and embroidered. Fabrics rely heavily on floral prints; subdued with plaids, stripes, and gingham in coordinating colors, accented with trims and fringes. No English Country room would be complete without at least one piece of furniture covered in chintz.

Formal

The White House is probably the country's best example of formal décor on public display. These interiors are noted for detailed and elegant features, such as high ceilings with plaster details, moldings, and furniture arranged in an orderly layout. Furniture pairs and matched sets with carved legs, tufted seats, pleated skirts and sophisticated lines grace the rooms. Most wooden surfaces, whether they be floors or furniture, are highly polished. Oriental rugs cover the floors. Sconces, lamps and chandeliers fashioned of brass and crystal illuminate the rooms. Sumptuous fabrics abound—damask, brocade, satin, velvet, and silk. Long, formal draperies made of flowing fabric embellish tall windows. Large works of art and mirrors encased in ornate frames give character to the walls.

French Country

Toile, checks, stripes and landscapes distinguish this time-honored look. Trademark landscape colors are comprised of brilliant shades of red, blue, yellow and green. French country artisans often hand-carve furniture from local cherry, pine and walnut. A classic example is the timeworn farm table that combines form with function. Picturesque landscapes are often the inspiration for French Country designs. Kitchen accessories utilize wrought iron hardware and hanging pot racks to emphasize rustic style. Architectural elements include glass-front cabinetry, large picture windows and arched door frames. One hallmark feature in the French Country kitchen is hand-painted tile of fruit, vegetables and herbs. A sanded, waxed plaster wall finishes the pastoral look.

Island/Tropics

If you've ever taken a vacation to Hawaii or the Caribbean, you already know the island theme: palm and parrot motifs, large floral prints, bamboo, sea life and torch lights. Wooden tables are carved with animals for legs, and furniture looks like it would be comfortable in the balmy heat. Tropical elements include: rattan, wicker, sea grass, linen, cottons, coco bark and raffia accents. Furniture is made from exotic woods, like koa, rosewood and teak. Bright colors prevail. Wall coverings, upholstery fabric and prints display tropical foliage—orchids, antherium, bird of paradise, plumeria and hibiscus.

Modern/Contemporary

Contemporary and all its variations is not for everyone, but fans like it for its clean lines, neutral components and bracing effect on their living space. It's all about lines and form. Color can be extremely bright, neutral or stark black and white punctuated with a specific color. Frequently the room features sculptures and modern art in unadorned frames. These rooms do not hide structural elements; rather they show off metal ductwork and ceiling pipes. The furniture is as simple as the room's space. That doesn't mean it has to be boxy, but it also doesn't allow for frilly fabrics, pastels or prim cloths. Flooring can range from painted concrete to wood to everything in between, as long as it's low maintenance and does not look fussy. Light is generated by recessed, indirect, track and one-of-a-kind lighting fixtures.

Romantic

Femininity rules this design. Many think of it as a lifestyle and place of comfort and retreat. The romantic look is equated with soft and graceful fabrics, laces, painted furniture, pastel colors, wispy curtains and fragrant flower arrangements. Colors range from cream to pink to powder blue to butter yellow. It's not necessary for every piece of furniture to match, but they should exhibit graceful curves, comfort and ease. Imagine yourself reading a book in an overstuffed chair or snuggled in a four-poster bed piled high with chenille coverlets and lace-edged pillows.

Rustic

If you've ever wanted to live in a log cabin or the mountains, this relaxed style is probably what you envisioned. It features large, rough-hewn, wood furniture upholstered in leather. Accessories include throw rugs and blankets, salvaged pine paneling, and earth and forest colors—greens, browns, rust, and golden tones. Art and fabric patterns abound with mountain animal motifs, such as moose, deer, wolves and wildcats. Coarse walls and exposed beams imbue log cabin life.

Southwestern

It's common for homes in the Southwest to bring the desert indoors. Rooms exude earth tones, rough textures, and brightly colored textiles. Architectural elements include adobe brick, hand-carved beams, uneven and rounded plaster walls, and kiva fireplaces with built-in niches for holding artifacts and crafts. These elements are highlighted by Indian accents and colorful woven rugs. Beamed ceilings crown the authentic Southwestern room. In the kitchen, dried chile braids hang from the walls, talavera tile lines the backsplash, Saltillo tile covers the floor, and rustic wood faces the cabinetry. Many Southwestern homes incorporate very old or locally carved doors made to look antique. Regional folk art like kachina dolls, carved animal sculptures and Indian pottery accessorize the home.

Tuscan

This look brings the Tuscan countryside into the home, giving its rooms a rural, yet cultured earthiness. These homes emulate a rustic, sun-baked look. All materials generate a feeling of warmth and old-world ambience. Colors range from gold to russet, pale beige, nut brown, olive green and terra-cotta—the hues of Tuscany's rolling hills. Accent colors abound in clear blues, dark leafy greens, vibrant reds and yellows. Stone predominates particularly in kitchens and baths, floors and walls. To get the most authentic look, most Tuscan-style homes feature limestone, granite and unpolished marble. Murals and trompe l'oeil work well with this style.

Victorian

Named after England's Queen Victoria, this style gained popularity during the second half of the 19th century. The affluence that accompanied the Industrial Revolution resulted in families having enough money to decorate every inch of their homes. Furniture was crowded into every room, knickknacks covered every tabletop, and highly embellished papers overlaid every wall. Today the style is characterized by intricate details and deep rich colors. Victorian furniture embodies dark finishes and elaborate carved designs. Oval chair backs, marble tabletops and dressers give elegance and import to rooms. Trims and fringe adorn rigid, upholstered furniture and drapes. Walls are covered with floral and highly patterned papers, while embossed paper is used to cover ceilings. These features are definitely fussy and formal, but are also perfect for the true Victorian home.

Western

Make a subtle statement with a few specific fabrics and cowboy-themed accessories like spurs on the walls. Or go over the top and make your room look like a kitschy Hollywood western out of the 1950s. Western fabrics, furniture and accessories have never been more popular. This style features a mix of woven materials including canvas, denim, Native American blankets and woolen area rugs, to natural materials of leather, rawhide, metal, and plank wood flooring. Large pieces of furniture, rough-hewed textures and Western-theme artwork play prominently in these rooms.

PICKING YOUR COLORS

Think about what colors you like. What colors make you happy and content? Which colors soothe your soul? Look in your closet and examine the dominant color you like to wear. Perhaps you wear a lot of red and blue, or maybe you own many outfits in taupe, chocolate and buff. Your clothes will tell you a lot about what colors you like.

There might be a piece of artwork in your home that you love. Look at the picture's colors. It could be that you're drawn to those colors.

Do certain colors make you anxious or agitated? If you loathe sage green, who cares what the trend is. You will hate your room if you paint or accent it in sage. Don't tell yourself you will learn to love it. Even if you do know exactly what you like, it's good to have an idea how colors work, or don't work, together. But before we get too far, become familiar with color lingo. A hue is a basic color, like yellow. Tone defines the color's density. Color value refers to the lightness or darkness of the hue. If white is added to a hue, a higher value tint is created. If black is mixed with a hue, a lower value shade is created. Saturation of a color refers to a color's purity or boldness.

Primary Colors
There are three pigments in traditional color theory: red, yellow and blue. These three colors cannot be mixed or created by any combination of other colors. These are known as the primary colors. Red, yellow and blue hues create all other colors.

Secondary Colors
If you mix red with blue, you get violet; red with yellow makes orange; and blue with yellow creates green. These are the secondary colors, which are made from the combination of two primary colors.

Tertiary Colors
The tertiary colors are a combination of a primary color and secondary color. Yellow-orange, red-orange, red-violet, blue-violet, blue-green and yellow-green.

Strive for color harmony in your project. There are three ways that colors work together in the most harmonious way. If you're wondering what harmony has to do with color, let's put it this way ... have you ever driven by a house painted the worst set of colors you've ever seen and asked out loud, "What was that person thinking?" Perhaps you've walked into someone's house and immediately felt uncomfortable. It may have been the color combination. When colors don't work together, they can create an unconscious level of discomfort. To avoid such a scenario, follow these methods for achieving color harmony:

Analogous

Any three colors that sit next to one another on a 12-part color wheel. For example, blue-green, blue, and blue-violet would be analogous. Usually one of the three colors predominates. In this case, it is blue.

Complementary

Any two colors directly opposite each other on the color wheel, such as yellow and violet. Opposing colors produce the greatest contrast and impression.

Triadic

This sounds more complicated than it is. Triadic means three high-energy colors that are separated by 120 degrees on the color wheel. Think of the wheel in thirds. For example, the primary colors of red, blue, and yellow, and secondary colors of violet, orange, green are triadic colors.

Natural

Who can argue with Mother Nature? If anyone knows how colors should work together, it's her. On the color wheel, red, yellow and green should not create a harmonious design, but in nature they do. Think of tulips with their red petals and yellow centers. Sometimes the colors found together in nature can inspire you to combine colors you may not have previously considered.

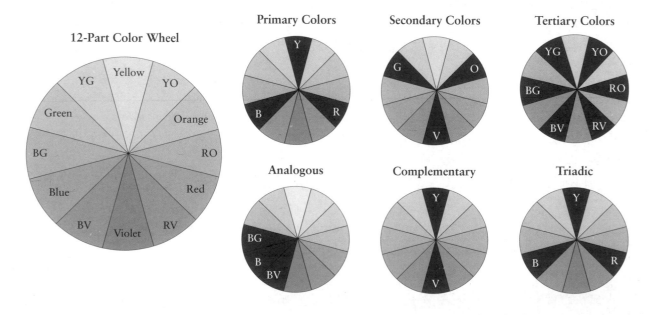

COLOR – THE GREAT ILLUSIONIST

Consider how color behaves in relation to other colors and shapes. Have you ever noticed that red appears more brilliant against a black background than a white one? Colors often look different depending on colors they appear next to. Keep this in mind when pairing colors.

Paint color can influence how the human eye perceives the size of a room. For example, dark tones of warm and cool colors tend to make a large room look smaller, which is great if you have an oversized room. But if you want a small room to look larger, stick with lighter colors on the ceilings, walls and floors. Be careful with dark walls and light floors. They create a floating effect. If you have dark walls and light floors, you don't want to counteract the effect with rugs or several large pieces of furniture.

Accent colors sustain the game of illusion. Paint the ceiling darker than the walls, and the ceiling will seem lower. Conversely a ceiling painted lighter than the walls makes the ceiling appear loftier and higher. To add a great look, you don't need to paint all the walls the same color. Paint one wall a shade darker or a shade lighter than the other walls. Depending on whether you go lighter or darker, you will create the illusion of more or less space. That wall will become the room's focus.

COLOR CHARACTERISTICS

Do colors possess characteristics? Can they influence mood? Many say they can, and that certain colors evoke emotions, while others downplay them. It's not a coincidence that many people paint their bedrooms a soothing blue. It's a calming color that helps people get to sleep and sets a soothing atmosphere for waking up in the morning. It's important to consider the mood that colors produce.

Active
Active colors are vibrant, warm colors, such as red, orange and yellow. They are vivid, bold and full of energy. These colors jump out at you. Use one of these colors to make an element stand out.

Passive
Cool colors, such as blue, green and violet are passive. They are soothing in nature and consequently soothe us in design. They calm, recede, and play a backseat role. Unlike active colors, they don't compete or shout.

Neutrals

These kinds of colors act as the benign area between active and passive. They are neither loud nor calm. Neutral colors include beige, brown, gray and white.

Pastel Colors

The softening of colors, made by adding a good deal of white, results in pastels. For some, pastels convey comfort, joy and the eternal look of spring. Others may look upon pastel colors as too modest and uninspiring.

Color Associations

- **Red** – passion, drama, sex, love, danger, desire, speed, strength, violence, anger, luck
- **Orange** – energy, warmth, balance, enthusiasm
- **Yellow** – friendship, joy, happiness, optimism, hope, sunshine, inspiration
- **Green** – nature, health, good fortune, renewal, youth, generosity, fertility
- **Blue** – tranquility, calm, stability, harmony
- **Violet** – nobility, spirituality, wisdom, enlightenment
- **Pink** – youth, femininity, romance, sensitivity
- **White** – purity, balance, simplicity, cleanliness, peace, innocence, winter, goodness
- **Black** – power, sophistication, wealth, fear, evil, mystery, sadness, remorse, anger, mourning and death

CHOOSING YOUR PERFECT COLORS

In general, rooms look complete when you utilize three different values: light, medium and dark. An all-light room can look too pallid, an all-medium room boring, and an all-dark room somber. Strive for a balance of all three.

Make a poster board of color swatches. At various times of the day see what the different swatches look like in the light. You might adore certain colors in the day, but during the evening under artificial light they might seem listless.

Better yet, pick out a few paint choices, brush them on large pieces of wood or plasterboard. Let them dry and lean them up against one of your room's walls. See what the color looks like throughout the day and evening. Make sure the boards dry completely, because paint is typically two shades darker after it dries. Move the boards around so you can see how the color will look in various places under different lighting conditions.

Do you have a sofa that you love? You can use it to create your color scheme. If it is multicolored, pull out the various colors in the fabric. For example, you have a couch that is predominantly chestnut with flecks of gold, red and hunter green. You could paint the walls a warm shade of gold, hang deep red window coverings and decorate the floors with hunter green rugs. But if the couch is just one color, you can still use it as a starting point. For example, a terra-cotta colored couch can be complemented with navy blue. This combo works because the colors lie opposite one another on the color wheel. Repeat the terra-cotta and blue in various tones throughout the room.

DECORATING DOS AND DON'TS

When picking out new furniture and wall coverings, make sure the scale and proportion matches your room. A too-large coffee table—while it might be gorgeous—can impede traffic, dent a few knees and dwarf other furniture. Wallpaper with a large pattern in a small room can overpower the space.

"The world is but a canvas to the imagination."
~Henry David Thoreau

WHEN PARTNERS DON'T AGREE

Psychologists and counselors often say that change can cause immense stress on a couple's relationship. Usually, they are referring to events like birth, death, illness, losing a job, getting a new job or moving. But as anyone who has gone through a home improvement project with a partner can tell you, remodeling should definitely be on this "stress" list. In fact, some people will assert it should crown the top of the list.

Why, you may wonder, should sprucing up your house be so stressful? It's quite simple. People are different. No two people think and react alike, no matter how compatible they are. We all have individual tastes. We each have the unique ability to visualize change. We have opinions on how to improve a living space. We have different ideas on how to handle projects and have different expectations for our "personal" space, for the place we call home. Just because you love someone doesn't mean you love that person's taste in Naugahyde upholstery.

It is often said that disagreements are nothing more than misunderstandings. That sounds great on the surface. You "understand" that your partner wants a brown corduroy easy chair in the living room. You just don't like it since you were envisioning an overstuffed wingback chair covered in rose-colored chenille. Understanding each other isn't going to easily close that design gap. Obviously the two of you have very different ideas for the room.

The first step is to agree to disagree. Recognize that what each of you wants is incompatible with what the other wants. Conflict isn't entirely bad. It forces you and your partner to seek new approaches that sometimes produce better results. If you have agreed to disagree, you've taken an important step, namely to communicate with each other. The next step is to negotiate. Both sides have to give a little and adjust until you both can reach an amicable agreement.

FIVE STEPS TO CONFLICT RESOLUTION

Start by practicing the fundamentals of conflict resolution. The following techniques are part of a proven problem solving system that has helped countless people just like you and your partner. These techniques can help you and your partner get through the disagreement and onto more important things, like accomplishing your home improvement project.

Step 1: Ground Rules

First, set some ground rules. Agree that you're going to truly work together toward an end result. Make a bargain that you're not going to stop until you get there. Be open-minded. Set some rules, such as not interrupting while the other is speaking, and no blaming or ridiculing the other one's ideas.

Step 2: Gather Perspectives

Second, gather perspectives. You accomplish this by listening. Each of you needs to be able to describe your needs, fears and viewpoints without interruption. Each of you must also listen without feeling defensive. Acknowledge that you heard what the other person said. The purpose is to understand what you each want and why. Be careful not to criticize the other's ideas or taste. Sincerely convey that you understand the importance of your partner's position just as your partner needs to sincerely understand yours. When partners truly understand and respect the other's point of view, each tends to be less guarded and more willing to listen to opposing opinions. For example, if you understand that your partner wants that corduroy chair because his deceased father had one like it, you might be more amenable to including it in the design. And if your partner understands that you grew up having to accept your older brother's masculine hand-me-downs, he might better understand why you want a more feminine look.

One caveat here: be genuine and don't fake sincerity. If your partner suspects that you are faking it to get him/her to see things your way, you not only won't resolve the conflict, but the process will become a great deal more difficult.

Step 3: Identify Common Interests

Third, identify common interests. Establish issues that are agreeable to both of you. Recognize what is important to each person. Emphasize the positives, and stay away from negatives that will begin the cycle of disagreement all over again.

Step 4: Seek Options

Fourth, seek options. List all possible solutions, even the most arcane ones. Think of options where everybody wins and plays fair. For example, perhaps you loathe Naugahyde but could easily live with leather. And maybe your partner actually prefers leather, but suggested Naugahyde to keep costs down. If you both agree that leather is a good compromise, you will easily resolve the issue.

Step 5: Agree on a Solution

Fifth, evaluate each person's perspective of the proposed solutions. Negotiate. Try to reach an agreement that is acceptable to both of you. When you reach an agreement, write it down.

As a motivating factor to keep the two of you on the road to compromise, imagine the consequence of not resolving the problem. Your home improvement project is at stake, which won't happen unless you both reach a cordial resolution. And if it doesn't happen because you both act stubborn and refuse to compromise, you will both be upset that you couldn't improve your home and are stuck living with it the way it is.

If you don't feel that you need to go the conflict resolution route, there is one other technique you might try that has proven successful. It's the Veto. Each of you gets a set number of design vetoes before you start planning your project. You both agree up front that if one of you truly hates a design or decorating element selected by the other, that person can use one of his or her "vetoes" and you will both honor that person's veto without question, comment or protest.

When that person reaches the maximum number of design vetoes agreed upon in advance, then he or she has to begin compromising. Using this technique, you both know you must choose your vetoes very carefully. It works best when the number of vetoes is limited. If it's a small project like a bathroom, limit the number of vetoes to a few, maybe five. With a larger project like a kitchen or addition, you might need more vetoes, say 10-15. This technique forces a couple to be careful, think through their choices and pick their battles.

.A few last thoughts to consider: During the negotiation process, keep all disagreements focused on the project. Don't allow them to get personal. Resolve to stay civil and respectful. After all, you live together and will continue to do so long after this project is finished. Just remember that your home belongs to both of you, regardless of who spends more time in the house.

Now get going on your project! Just think about how great your home will look when you and your partner are done. Stay focused on the future, and the present will take care of itself.

"Patience and perseverance have a magical effect
before which difficulties disappear and obstacles vanish."
~John Quincy Adams

WHEN PARTNERS DON'T AGREE

NOTES:

_____

_____

_____

_____

_____

_____

_____

_____

_____

_____

_____

_____

_____

_____

_____

_____

_____

_____

_____

_____

_____

_____

_____

_____

_____

_____

_____

_____

_____

BASIC INFORMATION AT-A-GLANCE

Maximize efficiency with the following organizational worksheets. Keep important phone numbers, email addresses and account numbers for all the key players in your renovation project in one place. Avoid flipping through pages of scrap paper, bids and margin notes to find that phone number you desperately need. It's helpful to have all the information you need in one accessible place in the event of an urgent situation. Try to be as thorough as you can when filling out the worksheets—later on you'll be thankful you did.

This section contains at-a-glance information for the following:

- Home Information
- Point-of-Purchase Contacts
- Recurring Service Providers
- Contractors
- Financial Information
- Other Monthly Expenses
- Home Improvement Budget

"At each increase of knowledge, as well as on the contrivance
of every new tool, human labor becomes abridged."
~Charles Babbage

HOME INFORMATION

HOME OVERVIEW

Date: _____   Move-In Date: _____

Square Footage: _____   Property Size: _____

Date Built: _____

DEVELOPERS/AGENTS

Name: _____

Phone: _____

Email: _____

PRIOR OWNERS

Name: _____

Phone: _____

Email: _____

WARRANTY INFORMATION

_____

_____

_____

_____

NOTES

_____

_____

_____

_____

_____

_____

POP Contact	Company Name	Primary Contact	Account/ Loan #'s	Company Address	Phone/ Fax #'s	Email Address
Primary Mortgage						
Secondary Mortgage						
Real Estate						
Homeowners Insurance						
Title Insurance						
Inspector/ Engineer						
Attorney						
Movers						
_____						
_____						
_____						
_____						
_____						
_____						
_____						

Service Provider	Company Name	Account #	Payment Address	Phone/ Fax #'s	Email Address	Website
Electric/ Energy						
Gas						
Oil						
Phone: Local						
Phone: Long Distance						
Water/Sewer						
Cable						
Internet						
Trash						
Exterminator						
Gardener						
Housekeeper						
Homeowners Association						

Contractor	Company Name	Primary Contact	Contractor Address	Phone/ Fax #'s	Email Address	Website
General Contractor						
Architect						
Designer						
Carpenter						
Decorator						
Electrician						
Landscaper						
Flooring Specialist						
Painter						
Plumber						
Roofer						
Exterminator						
Wallpaper Hanger						
Window Installer						
Drapery/Blinds Specialist						

FINANCIAL INFORMATION

HOME INFORMATION

Asked Price: _____ Purchase Price: _____

Appraisal Value: _____ Down Payment: _____

PRIMARY MORTGAGE

Lender: _____ Loan Number: _____

Billing Address: _____

City/State/Zip: _____

Phone: _____ Cell: _____

Email: _____

Loan Number: _____ Loan Amount: _____

Interest Rate: _____ Monthly Payment: _____

Terms (years, fixed, etc.): _____

Closing Costs: _____ Closing Date: _____

SECONDARY MORTGAGE

Lender: _____ Loan Number: _____

Billing Address: _____

City/State/Zip: _____

Phone: _____ Cell: _____

Email: _____

Loan Number: _____ Loan Amount: _____

Interest Rate: _____ Monthly Payment: _____

Terms (years, fixed, etc.): _____

Closing Costs: _____ Closing Date: _____

TOTAL MONTHLY EXPENSES

Principal & Interest Primary Mortgage: _____

Principal & Interest Secondary Mortgage: _____

Taxes and Other Fees: _____

Homeowners Association Fees: _____ Total Monthly Payment: _____

Expense	Budgeted	Actual
Electric/ Energy	$	$
Gas	$	$
Oil	$	$
Phone: Local	$	$
Phone: Long Distance	$	$
Water/Sewer	$	$
Cable	$	$
Internet	$	$
Trash	$	$
Exterminator	$	$
Gardener	$	$
Housekeeper	$	$
Homeowners Association	$	$

Total Monthly Cost: $ _____ $ _____

Project	Estimated Cost	% of Total Budget	Actual Cost

CONTRACTOR COMPARISON CHARTS

Contractors are the hired professionals who will perform the work on your home. In the event of a major renovation, the contractor will subcontract projects to other contractors. Many people select their own professionals to perform specific projects.

It can be difficult to choose the right contractors; that is why it is so important to rely on word-of-mouth recommendations, to visit the sites of completed projects and to check with your local Better Business Bureau and licensing entities for a track record of any contractors you are thinking about using.

The following charts will help you to compile valuable information in order to compare similar contractors side by side. This way, you will be able to view the pros and cons of each and decide which contractor best fits your needs. Once you make a selection, pertinent information will be already written in the grid for easy reference.

"Big results require big ambitions."
~Heraclitus

GENERAL CONTRACTOR COMPARISON CHART

DESCRIPTION OF PROJECT:

	Company 1	Company 2	Company 3
Company name			
Contact name			
Phone number			
Email			
License, bond, insurance information			
Workers: subcontractors or employees			
Workers' compensation & liability information			
Status with Better Business Bureau			
Years in business			
Warranties offered			
Number of current projects company is performing			
Replacement policy if a worker does not show (sick, vacation, etc.)			
Portfolio website			
Quoted price			
Project start date			
Estimated date of completion			

GENERAL CONTRACTOR COMPARISON CHART

	Company 1	Company 2	Company 3
Reference 1			
Phone number			
Comments			
Reference 2			
Phone number			
Comments			
Reference 3			
Phone number			
Comments			

ARCHITECT COMPARISON CHART

DESCRIPTION OF PROJECT:

	Company 1	Company 2	Company 3
Company name			
Contact name			
Phone number			
Email			
License, bond, insurance information			
Workers: subcontractors or employees			
Workers' compensation & liability information			
Status with Better Business Bureau			
Years in business			
Warranties offered			
Number of current projects company is performing			
Replacement policy if a worker does not show (sick, vacation, etc.)			
Portfolio website			
Quoted price			
Project start date			
Estimated date of completion			

	Company 1	Company 2	Company 3
Reference 1			
Phone number			
Comments			
Reference 2			
Phone number			
Comments			
Reference 3			
Phone number			
Comments			

DESIGNER COMPARISON CHART

DESCRIPTION OF PROJECT:

	Company 1	Company 2	Company 3
Company name			
Contact name			
Phone number			
Email			
License, bond, insurance information			
Workers' compensation & liability information			
Status with Better Business Bureau			
Years in business			
Warranties offered			
Number of current projects company is performing			
Replacement policy if a worker does not show (sick, vacation, etc.)			
Portfolio website			
Quoted price			
Project start date			
Estimated date of completion			

	Company 1	Company 2	Company 3
Reference 1			
Phone number			
Comments			
Reference 2			
Phone number			
Comments			
Reference 3			
Phone number			
Comments			

CARPENTER COMPARISON CHART

DESCRIPTION OF PROJECT:

	Company 1	Company 2	Company 3
Company name			
Contact name			
Phone number			
Email			
License, bond, insurance information			
Workers: subcontractors or employees			
Workers' compensation & liability information			
Status with Better Business Bureau			
Years in business			
Warranties offered			
Number of current projects company is performing			
Replacement policy if a worker does not show (sick, vacation, etc.)			
Portfolio website			
Quoted price			
Project start date			
Estimated date of completion			

	Company 1	Company 2	Company 3
Reference 1			
Phone number			
Comments			
Reference 2			
Phone number			
Comments			
Reference 3			
Phone number			
Comments			

DECORATOR COMPARISON CHART

DESCRIPTION OF PROJECT:

	Company 1	Company 2	Company 3
Company name			
Contact name			
Phone number			
Email			
Decorative style			
Status with Better Business Bureau			
Years in business			
Warranties offered			
Number of current projects company is performing			
Replacement policy if a worker does not show (sick, vacation, etc.)			
Portfolio website			
Quoted price			
Project start date			
Estimated date of completion			

	Company 1	Company 2	Company 3
Reference 1			
Phone number			
Comments			
Reference 2			
Phone number			
Comments			
Reference 3			
Phone number			
Comments			

ELECTRICIAN COMPARISON CHART

DESCRIPTION OF PROJECT:

	Company 1	Company 2	Company 3
Company name			
Contact name			
Phone number			
Email			
License, bond, insurance information			
Workers: subcontractors or employees			
Workers' compensation & liability information			
Status with Better Business Bureau			
Years in business			
Warranties offered			
Number of current projects company is performing			
Replacement policy if a worker does not show (sick, vacation, etc.)			
Portfolio website			
Quoted price			
Project start date			
Estimated date of completion			

	Company 1	Company 2	Company 3
Reference 1			
Phone number			
Comments			
Reference 2			
Phone number			
Comments			
Reference 3			
Phone number			
Comments			

LANDSCAPER COMPARISON CHART

DESCRIPTION OF PROJECT: _____

_____

_____

	Company 1	Company 2	Company 3
Company name			
Contact name			
Phone number			
Email			
License, bond, insurance information			
Workers: subcontractors or employees			
Workers' compensation & liability information			
Status with Better Business Bureau			
Years in business			
Warranties offered			
Number of current projects company is performing			
Replacement policy if a worker does not show (sick, vacation, etc.)			
Portfolio website			
Quoted price			
Project start date			
Estimated date of completion			

	Company 1	Company 2	Company 3
Reference 1			
Phone number			
Comments			
Reference 2			
Phone number			
Comments			
Reference 3			
Phone number			
Comments			

FLOORING SPECIALIST COMPARISON CHART

DESCRIPTION OF PROJECT: _____

_____

_____

	Company 1	Company 2	Company 3
Company name			
Contact name			
Phone number			
Email			
License, bond, insurance information			
Workers: subcontractors or employees			
Workers' compensation & liability information			
Status with Better Business Bureau			
Years in business			
Warranties offered			
Number of current projects company is performing			
Replacement policy if a worker does not show (sick, vacation, etc.)			
Portfolio website			
Quoted price			
Project start date			
Estimated date of completion			

	Company 1	Company 2	Company 3
Reference 1			
Phone number			
Comments			
Reference 2			
Phone number			
Comments			
Reference 3			
Phone number			
Comments			

PAINTER COMPARISON CHART

DESCRIPTION OF PROJECT: _____

_____

_____

	Company 1	Company 2	Company 3
Company name			
Contact name			
Phone number			
Email			
License, bond, insurance information			
Workers: subcontractors or employees			
Workers' compensation & liability information			
Status with Better Business Bureau			
Years in business			
Warranties offered			
Number of current projects company is performing			
Replacement policy if a worker does not show (sick, vacation, etc.)			
Portfolio website			
Quoted price			
Project start date			
Estimated date of completion			

	Company 1	Company 2	Company 3
Reference 1			
Phone number			
Comments			
Reference 2			
Phone number			
Comments			
Reference 3			
Phone number			
Comments			

PLUMBER COMPARISON CHART

DESCRIPTION OF PROJECT:

	Company 1	Company 2	Company 3
Company name			
Contact name			
Phone number			
Email			
License, bond, insurance information			
Workers: subcontractors or employees			
Workers' compensation & liability information			
Status with Better Business Bureau			
Years in business			
Warranties offered			
Number of current projects company is performing			
Replacement policy if a worker does not show (sick, vacation, etc.)			
Portfolio website			
Quoted price			
Project start date			
Estimated date of completion			

	Company 1	Company 2	Company 3
Reference 1			
Phone number			
Comments			
Reference 2			
Phone number			
Comments			
Reference 3			
Phone number			
Comments			

ROOFER COMPARISON CHART

DESCRIPTION OF PROJECT:

	Company 1	Company 2	Company 3
Company name			
Contact name			
Phone number			
Email			
License, bond, insurance information			
Workers: subcontractors or employees			
Workers' compensation & liability information			
Status with Better Business Bureau			
Years in business			
Warranties offered			
Number of current projects company is performing			
Replacement policy if a worker does not show (sick, vacation, etc.)			
Portfolio website			
Quoted price			
Project start date			
Estimated date of completion			

	Company 1	Company 2	Company 3
Reference 1			
Phone number			
Comments			
Reference 2			
Phone number			
Comments			
Reference 3			
Phone number			
Comments			

EXTERMINATOR COMPARISON CHART

DESCRIPTION OF PROJECT:

	Company 1	Company 2	Company 3
Company name			
Contact name			
Phone number			
Email			
License, bond, insurance information			
Workers: subcontractors or employees			
Workers' compensation & liability information			
Status with Better Business Bureau			
Years in business			
Warranties offered			
Number of current projects company is performing			
Replacement policy if a worker does not show (sick, vacation, etc.)			
Portfolio website			
Quoted price			
Project start date			
Estimated date of completion			

	Company 1	Company 2	Company 3
Reference 1			
Phone number			
Comments			
Reference 2			
Phone number			
Comments			
Reference 3			
Phone number			
Comments			

WALLPAPER HANGER COMPARISON CHART

DESCRIPTION OF PROJECT: _____

_____

_____

	Company 1	Company 2	Company 3
Company name			
Contact name			
Phone number			
Email			
License, bond, insurance information			
Workers: subcontractors or employees			
Workers' compensation & liability information			
Status with Better Business Bureau			
Years in business			
Warranties offered			
Number of current projects company is performing			
Replacement policy if a worker does not show (sick, vacation, etc.)			
Portfolio website			
Quoted price			
Project start date			
Estimated date of completion			

	Company 1	Company 2	Company 3
Reference 1			
Phone number			
Comments			
Reference 2			
Phone number			
Comments			
Reference 3			
Phone number			
Comments			

WINDOW INSTALLER COMPARISON CHART

DESCRIPTION OF PROJECT:

	Company 1	Company 2	Company 3
Company name			
Contact name			
Phone number			
Email			
License, bond, insurance information			
Workers: subcontractors or employees			
Workers' compensation & liability information			
Status with Better Business Bureau			
Years in business			
Warranties offered			
Number of current projects company is performing			
Replacement policy if a worker does not show (sick, vacation, etc.)			
Portfolio website			
Quoted price			
Project start date			
Estimated date of completion			

	Company 1	Company 2	Company 3
Reference 1			
Phone number			
Comments			
Reference 2			
Phone number			
Comments			
Reference 3			
Phone number			
Comments			

DRAPERY/BLINDS SPECIALIST COMPARISON CHART

DESCRIPTION OF PROJECT:

	Company 1	Company 2	Company 3
Company name			
Contact name			
Phone number			
Email			
License, bond, insurance information			
Workers: subcontractors or employees			
Workers' compensation & liability information			
Status with Better Business Bureau			
Years in business			
Warranties offered			
Number of current projects company is performing			
Replacement policy if a worker does not show (sick, vacation, etc.)			
Portfolio website			
Quoted price			
Project start date			
Estimated date of completion			

	Company 1	Company 2	Company 3
Reference 1			
Phone number			
Comments			
Reference 2			
Phone number			
Comments			
Reference 3			
Phone number			
Comments			

NOTES:

ROOM-BY-ROOM WORKSHEETS

Organization is your greatest weapon against the stress of renovating your home. The following pages break down your project room by room, and area by area, giving you lots of space to make your calculations and prepare for anything.

For each area of your home, there is a corresponding section in which you can list pertinent notes regarding the various elements that may be included. You'll soon find that the extensive information you enter into the organizer will become an essential reference throughout your entire renovation.

In each section, you will find an empty grid on which to lay out your ideas. The book includes furniture templates and room elements for you to play with to determine what works best for your space. You can also sketch in the grids if you have a more definite vision of your final outcome.

The more you plan and research ahead of time, the more you can enjoy the process of watching your home transform into a haven. If you fill in the pages to follow, you'll notice this book will become a companion you just can't live without during the renovation process.

FURNITURE TEMPLATES

All during the remodel process, you've been looking forward to the day when it's complete. You can't wait to furnish it and enjoy the new space. Chances are you have tons of ideas running through your mind about what will look right. Now is the time to give those ideas physical form. But before you even start shopping for furniture you should have a good idea about what will fit in your rooms and fulfill your needs.

HOW TO USE THE GRAPH PAPER AND FURNITURE TEMPLATES

Following each room section, you will find graph paper to help you lay out your space. Now take the measurements of your room (as it will be when completed), and draw your walls on the graph paper, noting the locations of doors (and the direction of the swing), windows, plumbing and electrical outlets. The scale is designed so that one grid square equals one square foot (1:1) or each line is equal to one linear foot. See the example on page 99.

Please note: For the furniture templates to reflect how your furniture will lay out in the actual space, be sure to follow the 1:1 scale provided. Measurements will be incorrect if you change the scale when using the furniture templates.

From this point you can measure all of your furnishings and items you want in the space. Pop out the furniture template corresponding to the approximate size of your furniture. Place the templates in the space you created on the grid paper. Move them around; experiment with how they fill the space. Do you have too much furniture, too little, or just the right amount? Check to make sure each item fits where you thought it would. Ensure lamps are placed close enough to an electrical outlet, and that nothing blocks the doors. It can be fun to see your rooms from a bird's eye view, and very helpful as well. Allow 3 feet between furniture for walking.

Now you can use the furniture templates located at the back of the book to lay out your room.

WHY THIS IS IMPORTANT

There are five good reasons to take the time to perform this essential exercise:

1. Functionality

The excitement of a room makeover sometimes skips over the practical aspect of how it will affect the functionality of a room. If the room has two or three entrances, will there be freedom of movement as people pass through, or is the configuration looking more like an obstacle course? If you want to remake the sitting area into a media room, is there enough space to install that 52-inch plasma television and still have sufficient room to sit at a comfortable distance from the screen? Graphically laying out the elements can avert disappointment when the job is done.

2. Proportion

A rough layout can tell you if your furniture is proportionate to the scale of the room. For example, if you have chosen delicate or minimalist furnishings, but the room includes high ceilings and an expansive addition, your furniture will be lost in the large room. Conversely, maybe you picked large overstuffed chairs and a large sofa, or maybe a sectional. Cramming these large pieces of furniture into a new smaller area will crowd the room. Sometimes, covering an entire wall with a custom cabinet solves storage and electronic equipment problems, but overpowers the rest of the room.

3. Space

This exercise can tell you if you have too many or too few furnishings in the room. Let's say you wanted that minimalist look in the new room. Placing the furniture templates of all the items you want in the room in a scaled representation of how the room will look when done helps you to immediately see if it will appear too 'cluttered' to convey a minimalist expression. Or, if you wanted the country or cottage look, you may discover you need a few additional pieces to adequately fill the space.

4. Requirements

This exercise can eliminate the "Oops!" factor. By noting on your drawing the precise location of all windows, doors (and which way the doors swing), vents in the floor, available power, and existing plumbing, you can situate furnishings the way you want without interfering with fixed elements. It may also indicate where additional power or plumbing will be required to suit your needs.

5. Ideas

Graphically laying out what you want to see can focus your thoughts. This is where the subtle "tweaking" of your ideas can save you a lot of frustration, time and money. It is not uncommon for the plan you ultimately adopt to differ from the first ideas that sparked your desire to improve your home. The more you refine your idea before involving the professionals, the more money you will save.

"Where we love is home, home that our feet may leave, but not our hearts."

~Oliver Wendell Holmes

MASTER BEDROOM

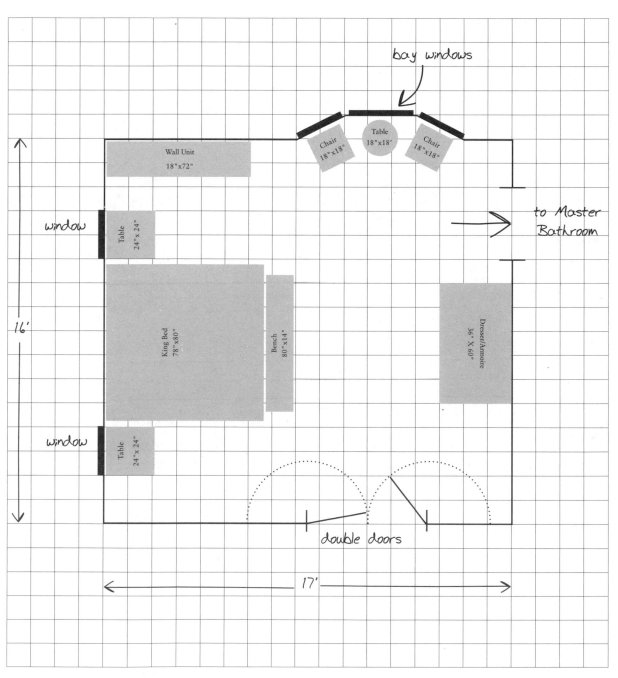

bay windows

Wall Unit
18"x72"

Chair
18"x18"

Table
18"x18"

Chair
18"x18"

window

Table
24"x 24"

to Master
Bathroom

16'

King Bed
78"x80"

Bench
80"x14"

Dresser/Armoire
36" X 60"

window

Table
24"x 24"

double doors

17'

1/4" measures 1'

DESCRIPTION OF PROJECT:

FLOOR	Dimensions:	Area:
Model:	Color/Style:	
Manufacturer:	Qty:	Material: $
Purchased From:		Date:
Warranty Info:		
Installer/Company:		Date:
Phone:	Cell:	Labor: $

PAINT	Dimensions:	Area:
Model:	Color/Style:	
Manufacturer:	Qty:	Material: $
Purchased From:		Date:
Warranty Info:		
Painter/Company:		Date:
Phone:	Cell:	Labor: $

WALLPAPER	Dimensions:	Area:
Model:	Color/Style:	
Manufacturer:	Qty:	Material: $
Purchased From:		Date:
Warranty Info:		
Installer/Company:		Date:
Phone:	Cell:	Labor: $

BASEBOARDS/TRIM/CROWN MOLDING		Length Required:
Model No:	Color/Style:	
Manufacturer:	Qty:	Material: $
Purchased From:		Date:
Warranty Info:		
Installer/Company:		Date:
Phone:	Cell:	Labor: $

LIGHTING/ELECTRICAL

Description	Manufacturer	Model/Style	Purchased From	Cost
				$
				$
				$
				$

Warranty Info:

Electrician/Company: Date:

Phone: Cell: Labor: $

DOORS/WINDOWS

Description	Dimensions	Manufacturer	Model/Style	Purchased From	Cost
Door 1					$
Door 2					$
Window 1					$
Window 2					$
Window 3					$
Window 4					$

Warranty Info:

Installer/Company: Date:

Phone: Cell: Labor: $

WINDOW/WALL COVERING

Description	Dimensions	Manufacturer	Model/Style	Purchased From	Cost
Window 1					$
Window 2					$
Window 3					$
Window 4					$
Wall 1					$
Wall 2					$

Warranty Info:

Installer/Company: Date:

Phone: Cell: Labor: $

LIVING ROOM

DECORATION/FURNITURE/FIXTURES

Description	Manufacturer	Model/Style	Purchased From	Cost
				$
				$
				$
				$
				$

Warranty Info:

Installer/Company: _____ Date: _____

Phone: _____ Cell: _____ Labor: $ _____

GENERAL CONSTRUCTION

Description	Cost
	$
	$
	$
	$
	$

Warranty Info:

General Contractor/Company: _____ Date: _____

Phone: _____ Cell: _____ Labor: $ _____

BUDGET ANALYSIS

Project	Budget	Actual Cost
Floor	$	$
Paint	$	$
Wallpaper	$	$
Baseboards/Trim/Crown Molding	$	$
Lighting/Electrical	$	$
Doors/Windows	$	$
Window/Wall Covering	$	$
Decoration/Furniture/Fixtures	$	$
General Construction	$	$
TOTAL	$	$

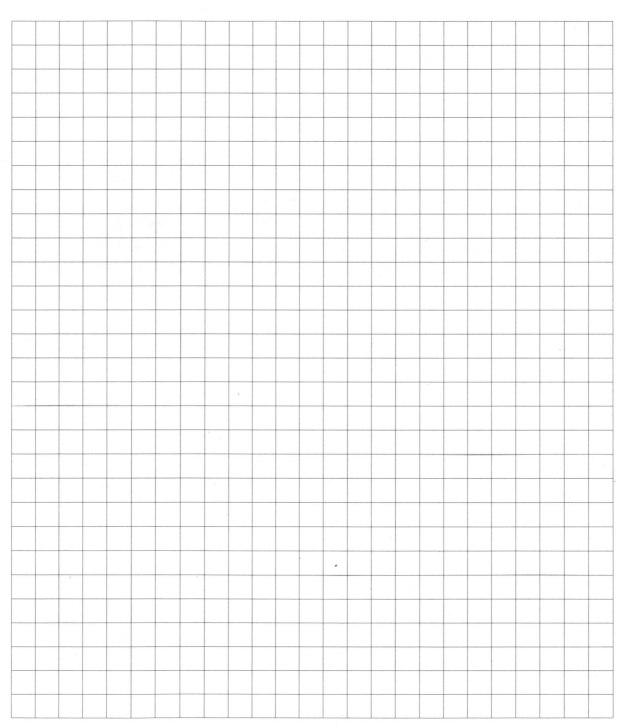

See pages 95-99 for an explanation on how to use this sheet.   1/4" measures 1'

DESCRIPTION OF PROJECT:

FLOOR	Dimensions:	Area:
Model:	Color/Style:	
Manufacturer:	Qty:	Material: $
Purchased From:		Date:
Warranty Info:		
Installer/Company:		Date:
Phone:	Cell:	Labor: $

PAINT	Dimensions:	Area:
Model:	Color/Style:	
Manufacturer:	Qty:	Material: $
Purchased From:		Date:
Warranty Info:		
Painter/Company:		Date:
Phone:	Cell:	Labor: $

WALLPAPER	Dimensions:	Area:
Model:	Color/Style:	
Manufacturer:	Qty:	Material: $
Purchased From:		Date:
Warranty Info:		
Installer/Company:		Date:
Phone:	Cell:	Labor: $

BASEBOARDS/TRIM/CROWN MOLDING		Length Required:
Model No:	Color/Style:	
Manufacturer:	Qty:	Material: $
Purchased From:		Date:
Warranty Info:		
Installer/Company:		Date:
Phone:	Cell:	Labor: $

LIGHTING/ELECTRICAL

Description	Manufacturer	Model/Style	Purchased From	Cost
				$
				$
				$
				$

Warranty Info:
Electrician/Company: Date:
Phone: Cell: Labor: $

DOORS/WINDOWS

Description	Dimensions	Manufacturer	Model/Style	Purchased From	Cost
Door 1					$
Door 2					$
Window 1					$
Window 2					$
Window 3					$
Window 4					$

Warranty Info:
Installer/Company: Date:
Phone: Cell: Labor: $

WINDOW/WALL COVERING

Description	Dimensions	Manufacturer	Model/Style	Purchased From	Cost
Window 1					$
Window 2					$
Window 3					$
Window 4					$
Wall 1					$
Wall 2					$

Warranty Info:
Installer/Company: Date:
Phone: Cell: Labor: $

DECORATION/FURNITURE/FIXTURES

Description	Manufacturer	Model/Style	Purchased From	Cost
				$
				$
				$
				$
				$

Warranty Info:

Installer/Company: _____ Date: _____

Phone: _____ Cell: _____ Labor: $ _____

GENERAL CONSTRUCTION

Description	Cost
	$
	$
	$
	$
	$

Warranty Info:

General Contractor/Company: _____ Date: _____

Phone: _____ Cell: _____ Labor: $ _____

BUDGET ANALYSIS

Project	Budget	Actual Cost
Floor	$	$
Paint	$	$
Wallpaper	$	$
Baseboards/Trim/Crown Molding	$	$
Lighting/Electrical	$	$
Doors/Windows	$	$
Window/Wall Covering	$	$
Decoration/Furniture/Fixtures	$	$
General Construction	$	$
TOTAL	$	$

See pages 95-99 for an explanation on how to use this sheet.   1/4" measures 1'

DESCRIPTION OF PROJECT:

FLOOR   Dimensions: Area:

Model: Color/Style:

Manufacturer: Qty: Material: $

Purchased From: Date:

Warranty Info:

Installer/Company: Date:

Phone: Cell: Labor: $

PAINT   Dimensions: Area:

Model: Color/Style:

Manufacturer: Qty: Material: $

Purchased From: Date:

Warranty Info:

Painter/Company: Date:

Phone: Cell: Labor: $

WALLPAPER   Dimensions: Area:

Model: Color/Style:

Manufacturer: Qty: Material: $

Purchased From: Date:

Warranty Info:

Installer/Company: Date:

Phone: Cell: Labor: $

BASEBOARDS/TRIM/CROWN MOLDING   Length Required:

Model No: Color/Style:

Manufacturer: Qty: Material: $

Purchased From: Date:

Warranty Info:

Installer/Company: Date:

Phone: Cell: Labor: $

CABINETS/STORAGE   Dimensions:

Model: Color/Style:

Manufacturer: Qty: Material: $

Purchased From: Date:

Warranty Info:

Installer/Company: Date:

Phone: Cell: Labor: $

COUNTERTOPS   Dimensions: Area:

Model: Color/Style:

Manufacturer: Qty: Material: $

Purchased From: Date:

Warranty Info:

Installer/Company: Date:

Phone: Cell: Labor: $

OTHER: Dimensions: Area:

Model: Color/Style:

Manufacturer: Qty: Material: $

Purchased From: Date:

Warranty Info:

Installer/Company: Date:

Phone: Cell: Labor: $

LIGHTING/ELECTRICAL

Description	Manufacturer	Model/Style	Purchased From	Cost
				$
				$
				$
				$
				$
				$

Warranty Info:

Electrician/Company: Date:

Phone: Cell: Labor: $

DOORS/WINDOWS

Description	Dimensions	Manufacturer	Model/Style	Purchased From	Cost
Door 1					$
Door 2					$
Window 1					$
Window 2					$
Window 3					$
Window 4					$

Warranty Info:

Installer/Company: Date:

Phone: Cell: Labor: $

WINDOW/WALL COVERING

Description	Dimensions	Manufacturer	Model/Style	Purchased From	Cost
Window 1					$
Window 2					$
Window 3					$
Window 4					$
Wall 1					$
Wall 2					$

Warranty Info:

Installer/Company: Date:

Phone: Cell: Labor: $

DECORATION/FURNITURE/FIXTURES/APPLIANCES

Description	Manufacturer	Model/Style	Purchased From	Cost
				$
				$
				$
				$
				$

Warranty Info:

Installer/Company: Date:

Phone: Cell: Labor: $

GENERAL CONSTRUCTION

Description	Cost
	$
	$
	$
	$
	$
	$

Warranty Info:

General Contractor/Company: | Date:

Phone: | Cell: | Labor: $

OTHER

Description	Manufacturer	Model/Style	Purchased From	Cost
				$
				$
				$
				$
				$
				$
				$
				$
				$
				$
				$
				$
				$
				$
				$
				$
				$
				$

Warranty Info:

Installer/Company: | Date:

Phone: | Cell: | Labor: $

KITCHEN

BUDGET ANALYSIS

Project	Budget	Actual Cost
Floor	$	$
Paint	$	$
Wallpaper	$	$
Baseboards/Trim/Crown Molding	$	$
Cabinets/Storage	$	$
Countertops	$	$
Lighting/Electrical	$	$
Doors/Windows	$	$
Window/Wall Covering	$	$
Decoration/Furniture/Fixtures/Appliances	$	$
General Construction	$	$
Other:	$	$
TOTAL	$	$

NOTES:

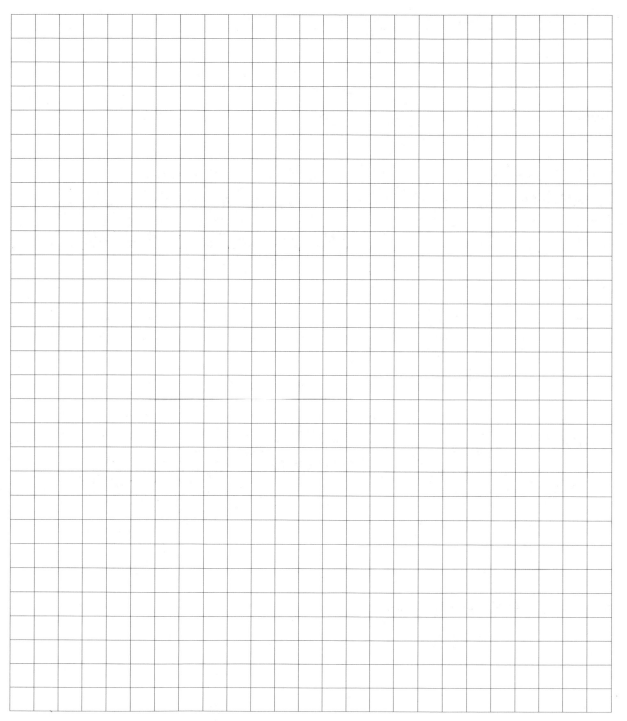

See pages 95-99 for an explanation on how to use this sheet.

1/4" measures 1'

DESCRIPTION OF PROJECT:

FLOOR   Dimensions: Area:
Model: Color/Style:
Manufacturer: Qty: Material: $
Purchased From: Date:
Warranty Info:
Installer/Company: Date:
Phone: Cell: Labor: $

PAINT   Dimensions: Area:
Model: Color/Style:
Manufacturer: Qty: Material: $
Purchased From: Date:
Warranty Info:
Painter/Company: Date:
Phone: Cell: Labor: $

WALLPAPER   Dimensions: Area:
Model: Color/Style:
Manufacturer: Qty: Material: $
Purchased From: Date:
Warranty Info:
Installer/Company: Date:
Phone: Cell: Labor: $

BASEBOARDS/TRIM/CROWN MOLDING   Length Required:
Model No: Color/Style:
Manufacturer: Qty: Material: $
Purchased From: Date:
Warranty Info:
Installer/Company: Date:
Phone: Cell: Labor: $

LIGHTING/ELECTRICAL

Description	Manufacturer	Model/Style	Purchased From	Cost
				$
				$
				$
				$

Warranty Info:

Electrician/Company: Date:

Phone: Cell: Labor: $

DOORS/WINDOWS

Description	Dimensions	Manufacturer	Model/Style	Purchased From	Cost
Door 1					$
Door 2					$
Window 1					$
Window 2					$
Window 3					$
Window 4					$

Warranty Info:

Installer/Company: Date:

Phone: Cell: Labor: $

WINDOW/WALL COVERING

Description	Dimensions	Manufacturer	Model/Style	Purchased From	Cost
Window 1					$
Window 2					$
Window 3					$
Window 4					$
Wall 1					$
Wall 2					$

Warranty Info:

Installer/Company: Date:

Phone: Cell: Labor: $

FAMILY ROOM

DECORATION/FURNITURE/FIXTURES

Description	Manufacturer	Model/Style	Purchased From	Cost
				$
				$
				$
				$
				$

Warranty Info:

Installer/Company: _____ Date: _____

Phone: _____ Cell: _____ Labor: $ _____

GENERAL CONSTRUCTION

Description	Cost
	$
	$
	$
	$
	$

Warranty Info:

General Contractor/Company: _____ Date: _____

Phone: _____ Cell: _____ Labor: $ _____

BUDGET ANALYSIS

Project	Budget	Actual Cost
Floor	$	$
Paint	$	$
Wallpaper	$	$
Baseboards/Trim/Crown Molding	$	$
Lighting/Electrical	$	$
Doors/Windows	$	$
Window/Wall Covering	$	$
Decoration/Furniture/Fixtures	$	$
General Construction	$	$
TOTAL	$	$

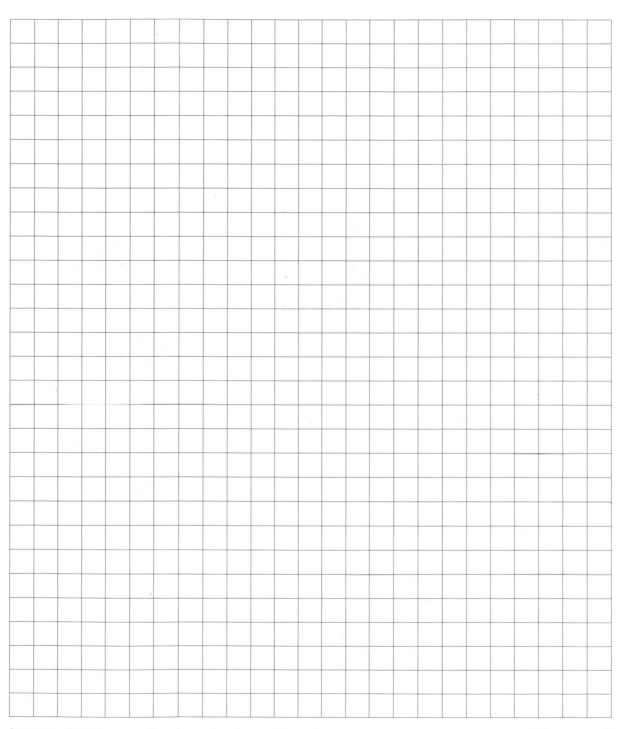

See pages 95-99 for an explanation on how to use this sheet.   1/4" measures 1'

DESCRIPTION OF PROJECT:

FLOOR   Dimensions: Area:
Model: Color/Style:
Manufacturer: Qty: Material: $
Purchased From: Date:
Warranty Info:
Installer/Company: Date:
Phone: Cell: Labor: $

PAINT   Dimensions: Area:
Model: Color/Style:
Manufacturer: Qty: Material: $
Purchased From: Date:
Warranty Info:
Painter/Company: Date:
Phone: Cell: Labor: $

WALLPAPER   Dimensions: Area:
Model: Color/Style:
Manufacturer: Qty: Material: $
Purchased From: Date:
Warranty Info:
Installer/Company: Date:
Phone: Cell: Labor: $

BASEBOARDS/TRIM/CROWN MOLDING   Length Required:
Model No: Color/Style:
Manufacturer: Qty: Material: $
Purchased From: Date:
Warranty Info:
Installer/Company: Date:
Phone: Cell: Labor: $

LIGHTING/ELECTRICAL

Description	Manufacturer	Model/Style	Purchased From	Cost
				$
				$
				$
				$

Warranty Info:

Electrician/Company: Date:

Phone: Cell: Labor: $

DOORS/WINDOWS

Description	Dimensions	Manufacturer	Model/Style	Purchased From	Cost
Door 1					$
Door 2					$
Window 1					$
Window 2					$
Window 3					$
Window 4					$

Warranty Info:

Installer/Company: Date:

Phone: Cell: Labor: $

WINDOW/WALL COVERING

Description	Dimensions	Manufacturer	Model/Style	Purchased From	Cost
Window 1					$
Window 2					$
Window 3					$
Window 4					$
Wall 1					$
Wall 2					$

Warranty Info:

Installer/Company: Date:

Phone: Cell: Labor: $

DECORATION/FURNITURE/FIXTURES

Description	Manufacturer	Model/Style	Purchased From	Cost
				$
				$
				$
				$
				$

Warranty Info:

Installer/Company: _____ Date: _____

Phone: _____ Cell: _____ Labor: $ _____

GENERAL CONSTRUCTION

Description	Cost
	$
	$
	$
	$
	$

Warranty Info:

General Contractor/Company: _____ Date: _____

Phone: _____ Cell: _____ Labor: $ _____

BUDGET ANALYSIS

Project	Budget	Actual Cost
Floor	$	$
Paint	$	$
Wallpaper	$	$
Baseboards/Trim/Crown Molding	$	$
Lighting/Electrical	$	$
Doors/Windows	$	$
Window/Wall Covering	$	$
Decoration/Furniture/Fixtures	$	$
General Construction	$	$
TOTAL	$	$

See pages 95-99 for an explanation on how to use this sheet.   1/4" measures 1'

DESCRIPTION OF PROJECT:

FLOOR   Dimensions: Area:

Model: Color/Style:

Manufacturer: Qty: Material: $

Purchased From: Date:

Warranty Info:

Installer/Company: Date:

Phone: Cell: Labor: $

PAINT   Dimensions: Area:

Model: Color/Style:

Manufacturer: Qty: Material: $

Purchased From: Date:

Warranty Info:

Painter/Company: Date:

Phone: Cell: Labor: $

WALLPAPER   Dimensions: Area:

Model: Color/Style:

Manufacturer: Qty: Material: $

Purchased From: Date:

Warranty Info:

Installer/Company: Date:

Phone: Cell: Labor: $

BASEBOARDS/TRIM/CROWN MOLDING   Length Required:

Model No: Color/Style:

Manufacturer: Qty: Material: $

Purchased From: Date:

Warranty Info:

Installer/Company: Date:

Phone: Cell: Labor: $

LIGHTING/ELECTRICAL

Description	Manufacturer	Model/Style	Purchased From	Cost
				$
				$
				$
				$

Warranty Info:

Electrician/Company: _____ Date: _____

Phone: _____ Cell: _____ Labor: $ _____

DOORS/WINDOWS

Description	Dimensions	Manufacturer	Model/Style	Purchased From	Cost
Door 1					$
Door 2					$
Window 1					$
Window 2					$
Window 3					$
Window 4					$

Warranty Info:

Installer/Company: _____ Date: _____

Phone: _____ Cell: _____ Labor: $ _____

WINDOW/WALL COVERING

Description	Dimensions	Manufacturer	Model/Style	Purchased From	Cost
Window 1					$
Window 2					$
Window 3					$
Window 4					$
Wall 1					$
Wall 2					$

Warranty Info:

Installer/Company: _____ Date: _____

Phone: _____ Cell: _____ Labor: $ _____

DECORATION/FURNITURE/FIXTURES

Description	Manufacturer	Model/Style	Purchased From	Cost
				$
				$
				$
				$
				$

Warranty Info:

Installer/Company: Date:

Phone: Cell: Labor: $

GENERAL CONSTRUCTION

Description	Cost
	$
	$
	$
	$
	$

Warranty Info:

General Contractor/Company: Date:

Phone: Cell: Labor: $

BUDGET ANALYSIS

Project	Budget	Actual Cost
Floor	$	$
Paint	$	$
Wallpaper	$	$
Baseboards/Trim/Crown Molding	$	$
Lighting/Electrical	$	$
Doors/Windows	$	$
Window/Wall Covering	$	$
Decoration/Furniture/Fixtures	$	$
General Construction	$	$
TOTAL	$	$

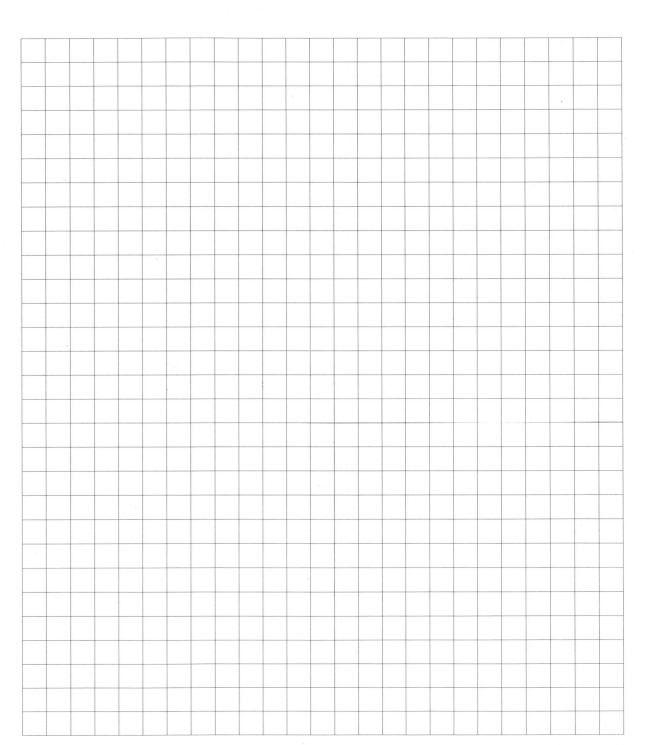

See pages 95-99 for an explanation on how to use this sheet.　　　　1/4" measures 1'

DESCRIPTION OF PROJECT:

FLOOR   Dimensions: Area:

Model: Color/Style:

Manufacturer: Qty: Material: $

Purchased From: Date:

Warranty Info:

Installer/Company: Date:

Phone: Cell: Labor: $

PAINT   Dimensions: Area:

Model: Color/Style:

Manufacturer: Qty: Material: $

Purchased From: Date:

Warranty Info:

Painter/Company: Date:

Phone: Cell: Labor: $

WALLPAPER   Dimensions: Area:

Model: Color/Style:

Manufacturer: Qty: Material: $

Purchased From: Date:

Warranty Info:

Installer/Company: Date:

Phone: Cell: Labor: $

BASEBOARDS/TRIM/CROWN MOLDING   Length Required:

Model No: Color/Style:

Manufacturer: Qty: Material: $

Purchased From: Date:

Warranty Info:

Installer/Company: Date:

Phone: Cell: Labor: $

LIGHTING/ELECTRICAL

Description	Manufacturer	Model/Style	Purchased From	Cost
				$
				$
				$
				$

Warranty Info:

Electrician/Company: Date:

Phone: Cell: Labor: $

DOORS/WINDOWS

Description	Dimensions	Manufacturer	Model/Style	Purchased From	Cost
Door 1					$
Door 2					$
Window 1					$
Window 2					$
Window 3					$
Window 4					$

Warranty Info:

Installer/Company: Date:

Phone: Cell: Labor: $

WINDOW/WALL COVERING

Description	Dimensions	Manufacturer	Model/Style	Purchased From	Cost
Window 1					$
Window 2					$
Window 3					$
Window 4					$
Wall 1					$
Wall 2					$

Warranty Info:

Installer/Company: Date:

Phone: Cell: Labor: $

DECORATION/FURNITURE/FIXTURES

Description	Manufacturer	Model/Style	Purchased From	Cost
				$
				$
				$
				$
				$

Warranty Info:

Installer/Company: Date:

Phone: Cell: Labor: $

GENERAL CONSTRUCTION

Description	Cost
	$
	$
	$
	$
	$

Warranty Info:

General Contractor/Company: Date:

Phone: Cell: Labor: $

BUDGET ANALYSIS

Project	Budget	Actual Cost
Floor	$	$
Paint	$	$
Wallpaper	$	$
Baseboards/Trim/Crown Molding	$	$
Lighting/Electrical	$	$
Doors/Windows	$	$
Window/Wall Covering	$	$
Decoration/Furniture/Fixtures	$	$
General Construction	$	$
TOTAL	$	$

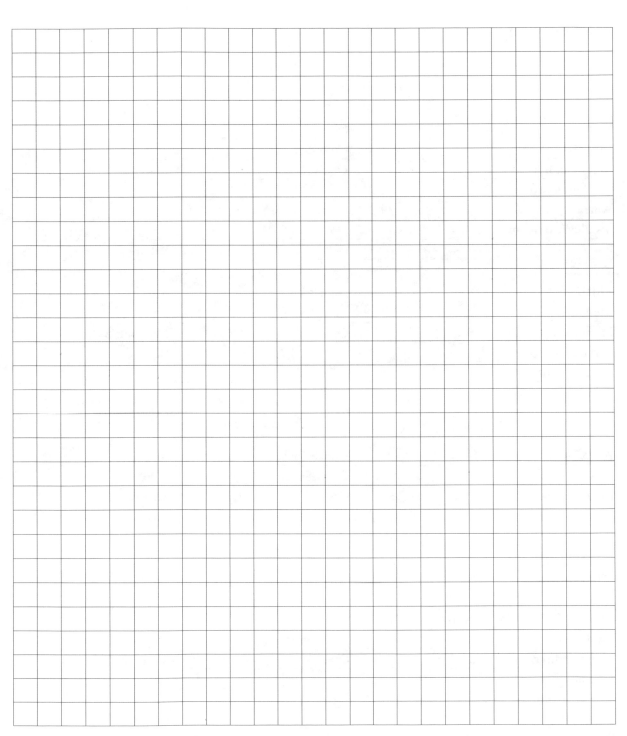

See pages 95-99 for an explanation on how to use this sheet.

1/4" measures 1'

DESCRIPTION OF PROJECT:

FLOOR   Dimensions: Area:

Model: Color/Style:

Manufacturer: Qty: Material: $

Purchased From: Date:

Warranty Info:

Installer/Company: Date:

Phone: Cell: Labor: $

PAINT   Dimensions: Area:

Model: Color/Style:

Manufacturer: Qty: Material: $

Purchased From: Date:

Warranty Info:

Painter/Company: Date:

Phone: Cell: Labor: $

WALLPAPER   Dimensions: Area:

Model: Color/Style:

Manufacturer: Qty: Material: $

Purchased From: Date:

Warranty Info:

Installer/Company: Date:

Phone: Cell: Labor: $

BASEBOARDS/TRIM/CROWN MOLDING   Length Required:

Model No: Color/Style:

Manufacturer: Qty: Material: $

Purchased From: Date:

Warranty Info:

Installer/Company: Date:

Phone: Cell: Labor: $

LIGHTING/ELECTRICAL

Description	Manufacturer	Model/Style	Purchased From	Cost
				$
				$
				$
				$

Warranty Info:

Electrician/Company: _____ Date: _____

Phone: _____ Cell: _____ Labor: $ _____

DOORS/WINDOWS

Description	Dimensions	Manufacturer	Model/Style	Purchased From	Cost
Door 1					$
Door 2					$
Window 1					$
Window 2					$
Window 3					$
Window 4					$

Warranty Info:

Installer/Company: _____ Date: _____

Phone: _____ Cell: _____ Labor: $ _____

WINDOW/WALL COVERING

Description	Dimensions	Manufacturer	Model/Style	Purchased From	Cost
Window 1					$
Window 2					$
Window 3					$
Window 4					$
Wall 1					$
Wall 2					$

Warranty Info:

Installer/Company: _____ Date: _____

Phone: _____ Cell: _____ Labor: $ _____

DECORATION/FURNITURE/FIXTURES

Description	Manufacturer	Model/Style	Purchased From	Cost
				$
				$
				$
				$
				$

Warranty Info:

Installer/Company: Date:

Phone: Cell: Labor: $

GENERAL CONSTRUCTION

Description	Cost
	$
	$
	$
	$
	$

Warranty Info:

General Contractor/Company: Date:

Phone: Cell: Labor: $

BUDGET ANALYSIS

Project	Budget	Actual Cost
Floor	$	$
Paint	$	$
Wallpaper	$	$
Baseboards/Trim/Crown Molding	$	$
Lighting/Electrical	$	$
Doors/Windows	$	$
Window/Wall Covering	$	$
Decoration/Furniture/Fixtures	$	$
General Construction	$	$
TOTAL	$	$

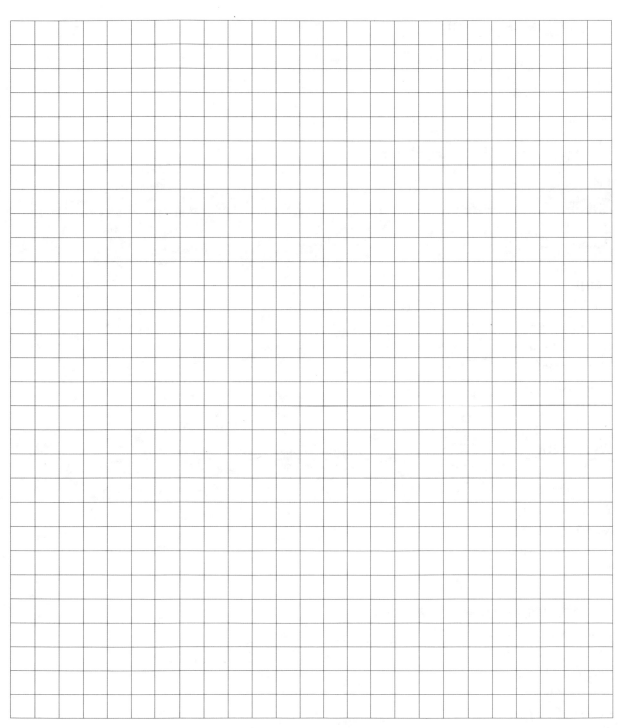

See pages 95-99 for an explanation on how to use this sheet.   1/4" measures 1'

DESCRIPTION OF PROJECT:

FLOOR   Dimensions: Area:

Model:	Color/Style:	
Manufacturer:	Qty:	Material: $
Purchased From:		Date:
Warranty Info:		
Installer/Company:		Date:
Phone:	Cell:	Labor: $

PAINT   Dimensions: Area:

Model:	Color/Style:	
Manufacturer:	Qty:	Material: $
Purchased From:		Date:
Warranty Info:		
Painter/Company:		Date:
Phone:	Cell:	Labor: $

WALLPAPER   Dimensions: Area:

Model:	Color/Style:	
Manufacturer:	Qty:	Material: $
Purchased From:		Date:
Warranty Info:		
Installer/Company:		Date:
Phone:	Cell:	Labor: $

BASEBOARDS/TRIM/CROWN MOLDING   Length Required:

Model No:	Color/Style:	
Manufacturer:	Qty:	Material: $
Purchased From:		Date:
Warranty Info:		
Installer/Company:		Date:
Phone:	Cell:	Labor: $

LIGHTING/ELECTRICAL

Description	Manufacturer	Model/Style	Purchased From	Cost
				$
				$
				$
				$

Warranty Info:

Electrician/Company: _____ Date: _____

Phone: _____ Cell: _____ Labor: $ _____

DOORS/WINDOWS

Description	Dimensions	Manufacturer	Model/Style	Purchased From	Cost
Door 1					$
Door 2					$
Window 1					$
Window 2					$
Window 3					$
Window 4					$

Warranty Info:

Installer/Company: _____ Date: _____

Phone: _____ Cell: _____ Labor: $ _____

WINDOW/WALL COVERING

Description	Dimensions	Manufacturer	Model/Style	Purchased From	Cost
Window 1					$
Window 2					$
Window 3					$
Window 4					$
Wall 1					$
Wall 2					$

Warranty Info:

Installer/Company: _____ Date: _____

Phone: _____ Cell: _____ Labor: $ _____

DECORATION/FURNITURE/FIXTURES

Description	Manufacturer	Model/Style	Purchased From	Cost
				$
				$
				$
				$
				$

Warranty Info:

Installer/Company: _____ Date: _____

Phone: _____ Cell: _____ Labor: $ _____

GENERAL CONSTRUCTION

Description	Cost
	$
	$
	$
	$
	$

Warranty Info:

General Contractor/Company: _____ Date: _____

Phone: _____ Cell: _____ Labor: $ _____

BUDGET ANALYSIS

Project	Budget	Actual Cost
Floor	$	$
Paint	$	$
Wallpaper	$	$
Baseboards/Trim/Crown Molding	$	$
Lighting/Electrical	$	$
Doors/Windows	$	$
Window/Wall Covering	$	$
Decoration/Furniture/Fixtures	$	$
General Construction	$	$
TOTAL	$	$

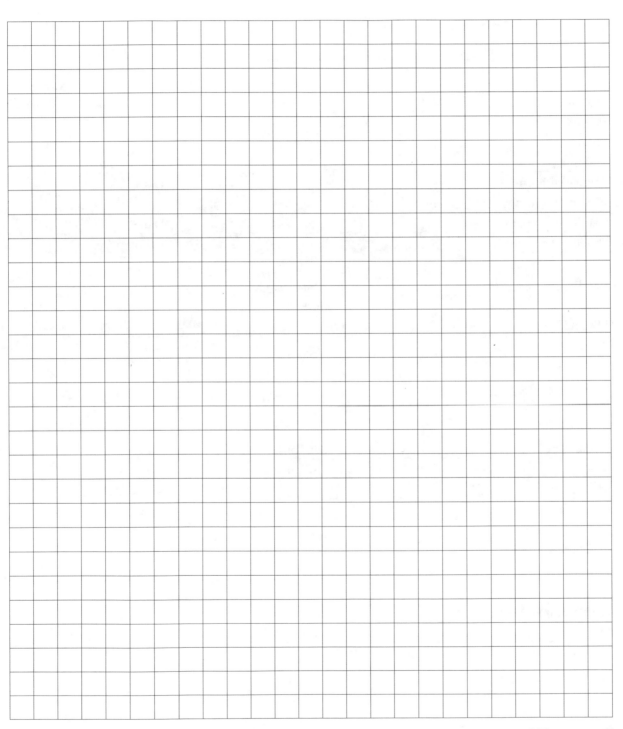

See pages 95-99 for an explanation on how to use this sheet.

1/4" measures 1'

DESCRIPTION OF PROJECT:

FLOOR   Dimensions: Area:

Model: Color/Style:

Manufacturer: Qty: Material: $

Purchased From: Date:

Warranty Info:

Installer/Company: Date:

Phone: Cell: Labor: $

PAINT   Dimensions: Area:

Model: Color/Style:

Manufacturer: Qty: Material: $

Purchased From: Date:

Warranty Info:

Painter/Company: Date:

Phone: Cell: Labor: $

WALLPAPER   Dimensions: Area:

Model: Color/Style:

Manufacturer: Qty: Material: $

Purchased From: Date:

Warranty Info:

Installer/Company: Date:

Phone: Cell: Labor: $

CABINETS/STORAGE   Dimensions:

Model: Color/Style:

Manufacturer: Qty: Material: $

Purchased From: Date:

Warranty Info:

Installer/Company: Date:

Phone: Cell: Labor: $

COUNTERTOPS

	Dimensions:	Area:
Model:	Color/Style:	
Manufacturer:	Qty:	Material: $
Purchased From:		Date:
Warranty Info:		
Installer/Company:		Date:
Phone:	Cell:	Labor: $

LIGHTING/ELECTRICAL

Description	Manufacturer	Model/Style	Purchased From	Cost
				$
				$
				$

Warranty Info:

Electrician/Company:	Date:
Phone: Cell:	Labor: $

DOORS/WINDOWS

Description	Dimensions	Manufacturer	Model/Style	Purchased From	Cost
Door 1					$
Window 1					$
Window 2					$

Warranty Info:

Installer/Company:	Date:
Phone: Cell:	Labor: $

WINDOW/WALL COVERING

Description	Dimensions	Manufacturer	Model/Style	Purchased From	Cost
Window 1					$
Window 2					$
Wall 1					$

Warranty Info:

Installer/Company:	Date:
Phone: Cell:	Labor: $

MASTER BATH

TUBS/TOILETS/SINKS/FIXTURES/DECORATION

Description	Manufacturer	Model/Style	Purchased From	Cost
				$
				$
				$
				$
				$

Warranty Info:

Installer/Company: Date:

Phone: Cell: Labor: $

GENERAL CONSTRUCTION

Description	Cost
	$
	$
	$
	$
	$

Warranty Info:

General Contractor/Company: Date:

Phone: Cell: Labor: $

BUDGET ANALYSIS

Project	Budget	Actual Cost
Floor	$	$
Paint	$	$
Wallpaper	$	$
Cabinets/Storage	$	$
Countertops	$	$
Lighting/Electrical	$	$
Doors/Windows	$	$
Window/Wall Covering	$	$
Tubs/Toilets/Sinks/Fixtures/Decoration	$	$
General Construction	$	$
TOTAL	$	$

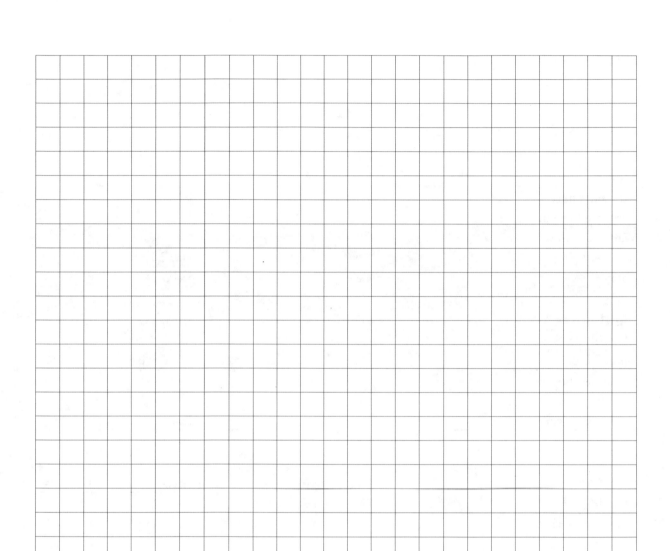

See pages 95-99 for an explanation on how to use this sheet.   1/4" measures 1'

DESCRIPTION OF PROJECT:

FLOOR   Dimensions: Area:

Model: Color/Style:

Manufacturer: Qty: Material: $

Purchased From: Date:

Warranty Info:

Installer/Company: Date:

Phone: Cell: Labor: $

PAINT   Dimensions: Area:

Model: Color/Style:

Manufacturer: Qty: Material: $

Purchased From: Date:

Warranty Info:

Painter/Company: Date:

Phone: Cell: Labor: $

WALLPAPER   Dimensions: Area:

Model: Color/Style:

Manufacturer: Qty: Material: $

Purchased From: Date:

Warranty Info:

Installer/Company: Date:

Phone: Cell: Labor: $

CABINETS/STORAGE   Dimensions:

Model: Color/Style:

Manufacturer: Qty: Material: $

Purchased From: Date:

Warranty Info:

Installer/Company: Date:

Phone: Cell: Labor: $

COUNTERTOPS

	Dimensions:	Area:
Model:	Color/Style:	
Manufacturer:	Qty:	Material: $
Purchased From:		Date:
Warranty Info:		
Installer/Company:		Date:
Phone:	Cell:	Labor: $

LIGHTING/ELECTRICAL

Description	Manufacturer	Model/Style	Purchased From	Cost
				$
				$
				$

Warranty Info:

Electrician/Company:		Date:
Phone:	Cell:	Labor: $

DOORS/WINDOWS

Description	Dimensions	Manufacturer	Model/Style	Purchased From	Cost
Door 1					$
Window 1					$
Window 2					$

Warranty Info:

Installer/Company:		Date:
Phone:	Cell:	Labor: $

WINDOW/WALL COVERING

Description	Dimensions	Manufacturer	Model/Style	Purchased From	Cost
Window 1					$
Window 2					$
Wall 1					$

Warranty Info:

Installer/Company:		Date:
Phone:	Cell:	Labor: $

TUBS/TOILETS/SINKS/FIXTURES/DECORATION

Description	Manufacturer	Model/Style	Purchased From	Cost
				$
				$
				$
				$
				$

Warranty Info:

Installer/Company: Date:

Phone: Cell: Labor: $

GENERAL CONSTRUCTION

Description	Cost
	$
	$
	$
	$
	$

Warranty Info:

General Contractor/Company: Date:

Phone: Cell: Labor: $

BUDGET ANALYSIS

Project	Budget	Actual Cost
Floor	$	$
Paint	$	$
Wallpaper	$	$
Cabinets/Storage	$	$
Countertops	$	$
Lighting/Electrical	$	$
Doors/Windows	$	$
Window/Wall Covering	$	$
Tubs/Toilets/Sinks/Fixtures/Decoration	$	$
General Construction	$	$
TOTAL	$	$

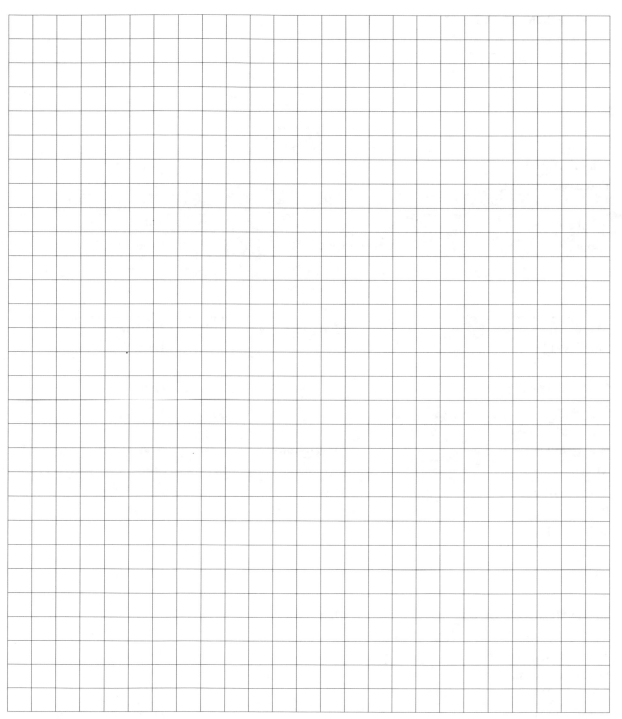

See pages 95-99 for an explanation on how to use this sheet.   1/4" measures 1'

DESCRIPTION OF PROJECT:

FLOOR	Dimensions:	Area:
Model:	Color/Style:	
Manufacturer:	Qty:	Material: $
Purchased From:		Date:
Warranty Info:		
Installer/Company:		Date:
Phone:	Cell:	Labor: $

PAINT	Dimensions:	Area:
Model:	Color/Style:	
Manufacturer:	Qty:	Material: $
Purchased From:		Date:
Warranty Info:		
Painter/Company:		Date:
Phone:	Cell:	Labor: $

WALLPAPER	Dimensions:	Area:
Model:	Color/Style:	
Manufacturer:	Qty:	Material: $
Purchased From:		Date:
Warranty Info:		
Installer/Company:		Date:
Phone:	Cell:	Labor: $

CABINETS/STORAGE	Dimensions:	
Model:	Color/Style:	
Manufacturer:	Qty:	Material: $
Purchased From:		Date:
Warranty Info:		
Installer/Company:		Date:
Phone:	Cell:	Labor: $

COUNTERTOPS

	Dimensions:	Area:
Model:	Color/Style:	
Manufacturer:	Qty:	Material: $
Purchased From:		Date:
Warranty Info:		
Installer/Company:		Date:
Phone:	Cell:	Labor: $

LIGHTING/ELECTRICAL

Description	Manufacturer	Model/Style	Purchased From	Cost
				$
				$
				$

Warranty Info:

Electrician/Company: Date:

Phone: Cell: Labor: $

DOORS/WINDOWS

Description	Dimensions	Manufacturer	Model/Style	Purchased From	Cost
Door 1					$
Window 1					$
Window 2					$

Warranty Info:

Installer/Company: Date:

Phone: Cell: Labor: $

WINDOW/WALL COVERING

Description	Dimensions	Manufacturer	Model/Style	Purchased From	Cost
Window 1					$
Window 2					$
Wall 1					$

Warranty Info:

Installer/Company: Date:

Phone: Cell: Labor: $

TUBS/TOILETS/SINKS/FIXTURES/DECORATION

Description	Manufacturer	Model/Style	Purchased From	Cost
				$
				$
				$
				$
				$

Warranty Info:

Installer/Company: Date:

Phone: Cell: Labor: $

GENERAL CONSTRUCTION

Description	Cost
	$
	$
	$
	$
	$

Warranty Info:

General Contractor/Company: Date:

Phone: Cell: Labor: $

BUDGET ANALYSIS

Project	Budget	Actual Cost
Floor	$	$
Paint	$	$
Wallpaper	$	$
Cabinets/Storage	$	$
Countertops	$	$
Lighting/Electrical	$	$
Doors/Windows	$	$
Window/Wall Covering	$	$
Tubs/Toilets/Sinks/Fixtures/Decoration	$	$
General Construction	$	$
TOTAL	$	$

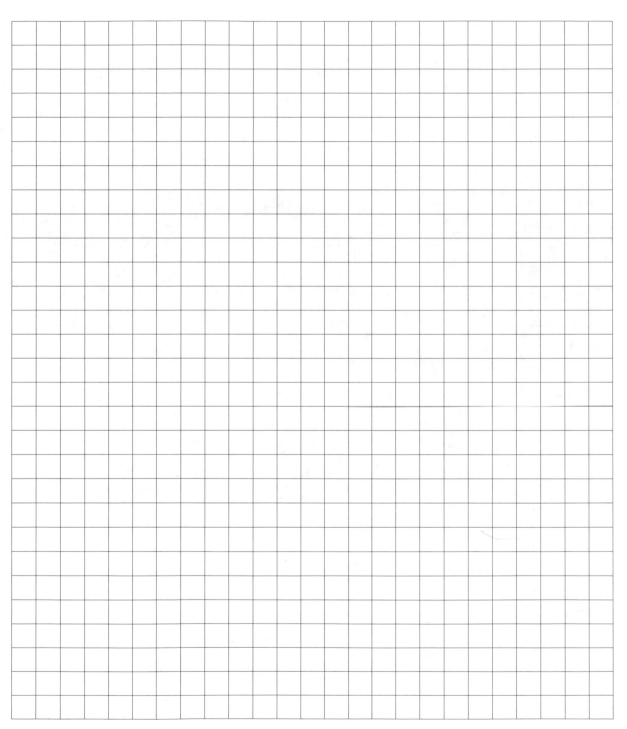

See pages 95-99 for an explanation on how to use this sheet.   1/4" measures 1'

DESCRIPTION OF PROJECT:

FLOOR   Dimensions: Area:

Model: Color/Style:

Manufacturer: Qty: Material: $

Purchased From: Date:

Warranty Info:

Installer/Company: Date:

Phone: Cell: Labor: $

PAINT   Dimensions: Area:

Model: Color/Style:

Manufacturer: Qty: Material: $

Purchased From: Date:

Warranty Info:

Painter/Company: Date:

Phone: Cell: Labor: $

CABINETS/STORAGE   Dimensions:

Model: Color/Style:

Manufacturer: Qty: Material: $

Purchased From: Date:

Warranty Info:

Installer/Company: Date:

Phone: Cell: Labor: $

COUNTERTOPS   Dimensions: Area:

Model: Color/Style:

Manufacturer: Qty: Material: $

Purchased From: Date:

Warranty Info:

Installer/Company: Date:

Phone: Cell: Labor: $

LIGHTING/ELECTRICAL

Description	Manufacturer	Model/Style	Purchased From	Cost
				$
				$
				$
				$

Warranty Info:

Electrician/Company: Date:

Phone: Cell: Labor: $

DOORS/WINDOWS

Description	Dimensions	Manufacturer	Model/Style	Purchased From	Cost
Door 1					$
Door 2					$
Window 1					$
Window 2					$
Window 3					$
Window 4					$

Warranty Info:

Installer/Company: Date:

Phone: Cell: Labor: $

WINDOW/WALL COVERING

Description	Dimensions	Manufacturer	Model/Style	Purchased From	Cost
Window 1					$
Window 2					$
Window 3					$
Window 4					$
Wall 1					$
Wall 2					$

Warranty Info:

Installer/Company: Date:

Phone: Cell: Labor: $

WASHER/DRYER/FIXTURES/APPLIANCES

Description	Manufacturer	Model/Style	Purchased From	Cost
				$
				$
				$
				$
				$

Warranty Info:

Installer/Company: Date:

Phone: Cell: Labor: $

GENERAL CONSTRUCTION

Description	Cost
	$
	$
	$
	$
	$

Warranty Info:

General Contractor/Company: Date:

Phone: Cell: Labor: $

BUDGET ANALYSIS

Project	Budget	Actual Cost
Floor	$	$
Paint	$	$
Cabinets/Storage	$	$
Countertops	$	$
Lighting/Electrical	$	$
Doors/Windows	$	$
Window/Wall Covering	$	$
Washer/Dryer/Fixtures/Appliances	$	$
General Construction	$	$
TOTAL	$	$

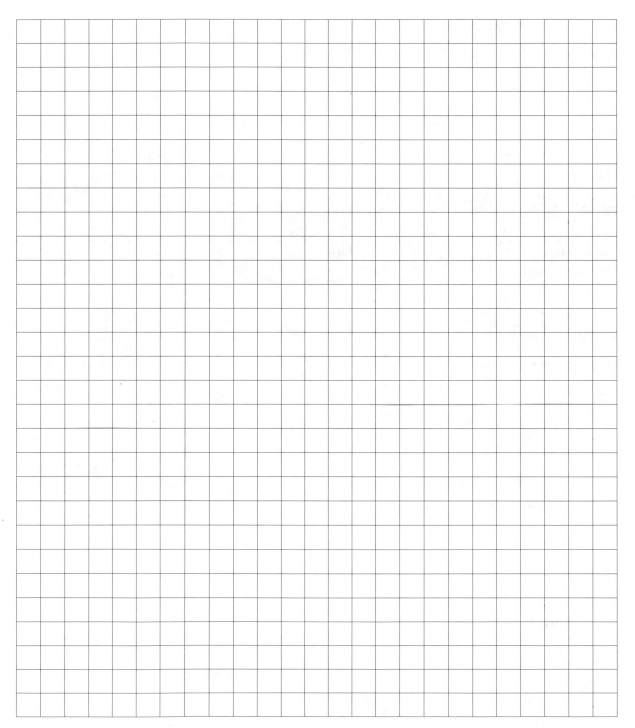

See pages 95-99 for an explanation on how to use this sheet.   1/4" measures 1'

ATTIC

DESCRIPTION OF PROJECT:

FLOOR	Dimensions:	Area:
Model:	Color/Style:	
Manufacturer:	Qty:	Material: $
Purchased From:		Date:
Warranty Info:		
Installer/Company:		Date:
Phone:	Cell:	Labor: $

PAINT	Dimensions:	Area:
Model:	Color/Style:	
Manufacturer:	Qty:	Material: $
Purchased From:		Date:
Warranty Info:		
Painter/Company:		Date:
Phone:	Cell:	Labor: $

LIGHTING/ELECTRICAL

Description	Manufacturer	Model/Style	Purchased From	Cost
				$

Warranty Info:

Electrician/Company:		Date:
Phone:	Cell:	Labor: $

GENERAL CONSTRUCTION

Description:	Cost: $
Warranty Info:	
General Contractor/Company:	Installation Date:
Phone:	Cell:

BUDGET ANALYSIS

Project	Budget	Actual Cost
Floor	$	$
Paint	$	$
Lighting/Electrical	$	$
General Construction	$	$
TOTAL	$	$

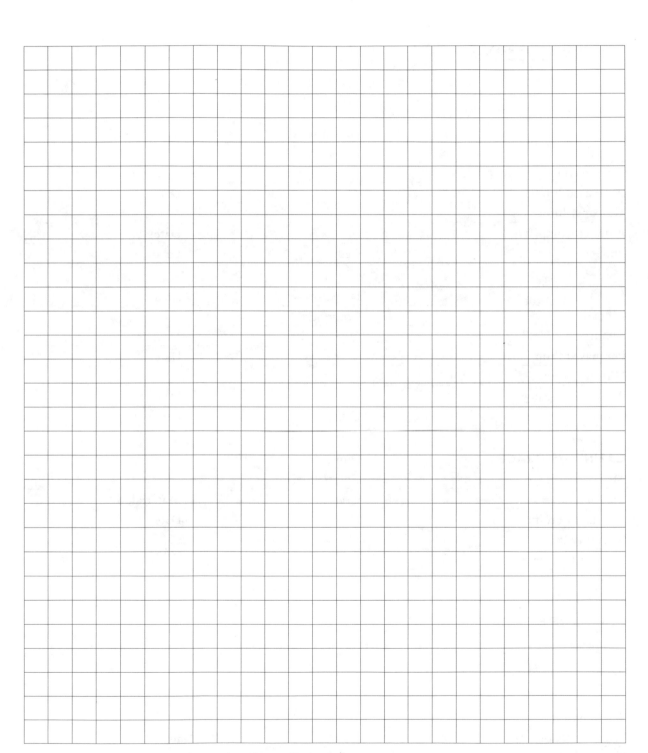

See pages 95-99 for an explanation on how to use this sheet.

1/4" measures 1'

DESCRIPTION OF PROJECT:

FLOOR   Dimensions: Area:

Model: Color/Style:

Manufacturer: Qty: Material: $

Purchased From: Date:

Warranty Info:

Installer/Company: Date:

Phone: Cell: Labor: $

PAINT   Dimensions: Area:

Model: Color/Style:

Manufacturer: Qty: Material: $

Purchased From: Date:

Warranty Info:

Painter/Company: Date:

Phone: Cell: Labor: $

CABINETS/STORAGE   Dimensions:

Model: Color/Style:

Manufacturer: Qty: Material: $

Purchased From: Date:

Warranty Info:

Installer/Company: Date:

Phone: Cell: Labor: $

LIGHTING/ELECTRICAL

Description	Manufacturer	Model/Style	Purchased From	Cost
				$
				$

Warranty Info:

Electrician/Company: Date:

Phone: Cell: Labor: $

DOORS/WINDOWS

Description	Dimensions	Manufacturer	Model/Style	Purchased From	Cost
Door 1					$
Door 2					$
Window 1					$
Window 2					$
Window 3					$
Window 4					$

Warranty Info:

Installer/Company: Date:

Phone: Cell: Labor: $

WINDOW/WALL COVERING

Description	Dimensions	Manufacturer	Model/Style	Purchased From	Cost
Window 1					$
Window 2					$
Window 3					$
Window 4					$
Wall 1					$
Wall 2					$

Warranty Info:

Installer/Company: Date:

Phone: Cell: Labor: $

FURNITURE/FIXTURES/APPLIANCES

Description	Manufacturer	Model/Style	Purchased From	Cost
				$
				$
				$
				$
				$

Warranty Info:

Installer/Company: Date:

Phone: Cell: Labor: $

BASEMENT

GENERAL CONSTRUCTION

Description	Cost
	$
	$
	$
	$

Warranty Info:

General Contractor/Company: Date:

Phone: Cell: Labor: $

BUDGET ANALYSIS

Project	Budget	Actual Cost
Floor	$	$
Paint	$	$
Cabinets/Storage	$	$
Lighting/Electrical	$	$
Doors/Windows	$	$
Window/Wall Covering	$	$
Furniture/Fixtures/Appliances	$	$
General Construction	$	$
TOTAL	$	$

NOTES:

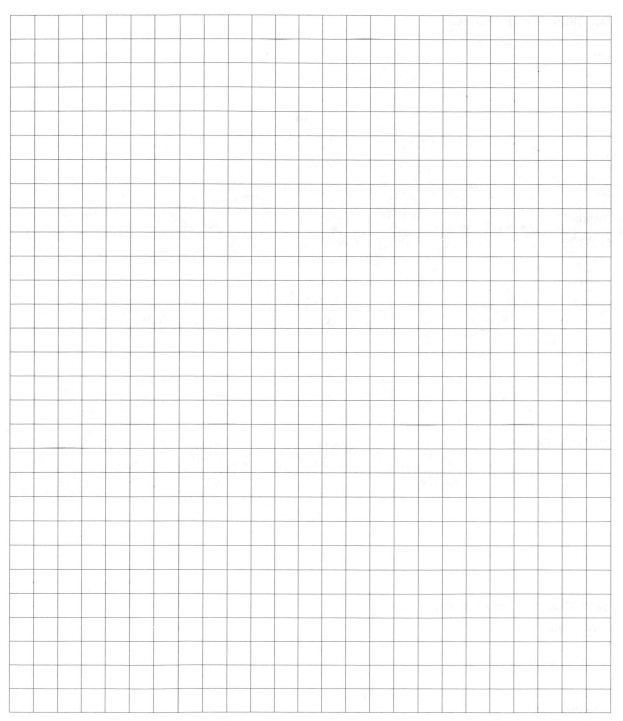

See pages 95-99 for an explanation on how to use this sheet.   1/4" measures 1'

OTHER ROOMS

Make copies of the following pages of this section as necessary for any additional rooms.

DESCRIPTION OF PROJECT:

FLOOR — Dimensions: — Area:
Model: — Color/Style:
Manufacturer: — Qty: — Material: $
Purchased From: — Date:
Warranty Info:
Installer/Company: — Date:
Phone: — Cell: — Labor: $

PAINT — Dimensions: — Area:
Model: — Color/Style:
Manufacturer: — Qty: — Material: $
Purchased From: — Date:
Warranty Info:
Painter/Company: — Date:
Phone: — Cell: — Labor: $

WALLPAPER — Dimensions: — Area:
Model: — Color/Style:
Manufacturer: — Qty: — Material: $
Purchased From: — Date:
Warranty Info:
Installer/Company: — Date:
Phone: — Cell: — Labor: $

BASEBOARDS/TRIM/CROWN MOLDING — Length Required:
Model No: — Color/Style:
Manufacturer: — Qty: — Material: $
Purchased From: — Date:
Warranty Info:
Installer/Company: — Date:
Phone: — Cell: — Labor: $

CABINETS/STORAGE

	Dimensions:	
Model:	Color/Style:	
Manufacturer:	Qty:	Material: $
Purchased From:		Date:
Warranty Info:		
Installer/Company:		Date:
Phone:	Cell:	Labor: $

COUNTERTOPS

	Dimensions:	Area:
Model:	Color/Style:	
Manufacturer:	Qty:	Material: $
Purchased From:		Date:
Warranty Info:		
Installer/Company:		Date:
Phone:	Cell:	Labor: $

OTHER:

	Dimensions:	Area:
Model:	Color/Style:	
Manufacturer:	Qty:	Material: $
Purchased From:		Date:
Warranty Info:		
Installer/Company:		Date:
Phone:	Cell:	Labor: $

LIGHTING/ELECTRICAL

Description	Manufacturer	Model/Style	Purchased From	Cost
				$
				$
				$
				$
				$

Warranty Info:

Electrician/Company: Date:

Phone: Cell: Labor: $

DOORS/WINDOWS

Description	Dimensions	Manufacturer	Model/Style	Purchased From	Cost
Door 1					$
Door 2					$
Window 1					$
Window 2					$
Window 3					$
Window 4					$

Warranty Info:

Installer/Company: Date:

Phone: Cell: Labor: $

WINDOW/WALL COVERING

Description	Dimensions	Manufacturer	Model/Style	Purchased From	Cost
Window 1					$
Window 2					$
Window 3					$
Window 4					$
Wall 1					$
Wall 2					$

Warranty Info:

Installer/Company: Date:

Phone: Cell: Labor: $

DECORATION/FURNITURE/FIXTURES/APPLIANCES

Description	Manufacturer	Model/Style	Purchased From	Cost
				$
				$
				$
				$
				$

Warranty Info:

Installer/Company: Date:

Phone: Cell: Labor: $

GENERAL CONSTRUCTION

Description	Cost
	$
	$
	$
	$
	$
	$
	$
	$
	$
	$
	$

Warranty Info:

General Contractor/Company: _____ Date: _____

Phone: _____ Cell: _____ Labor: $ _____

OTHER

Description	Cost
	$
	$
	$
	$
	$
	$
	$
	$
	$
	$
	$
	$

Warranty Info:

Installer/Company: _____ Date: _____

Phone: _____ Cell: _____ Labor: $ _____

BUDGET ANALYSIS

Project	Budget	Actual Cost
Floor	$	$
Paint	$	$
Wallpaper	$	$
Baseboards/Trim/Crown Molding	$	$
Cabinets/Storage	$	$
Countertops	$	$
Lighting/Electrical	$	$
Doors/Windows	$	$
Window/Wall Covering	$	$
Decoration/Furniture/Fixtures/Appliances	$	$
General Construction	$	$
Other:	$	$
TOTAL	$	$

NOTES:

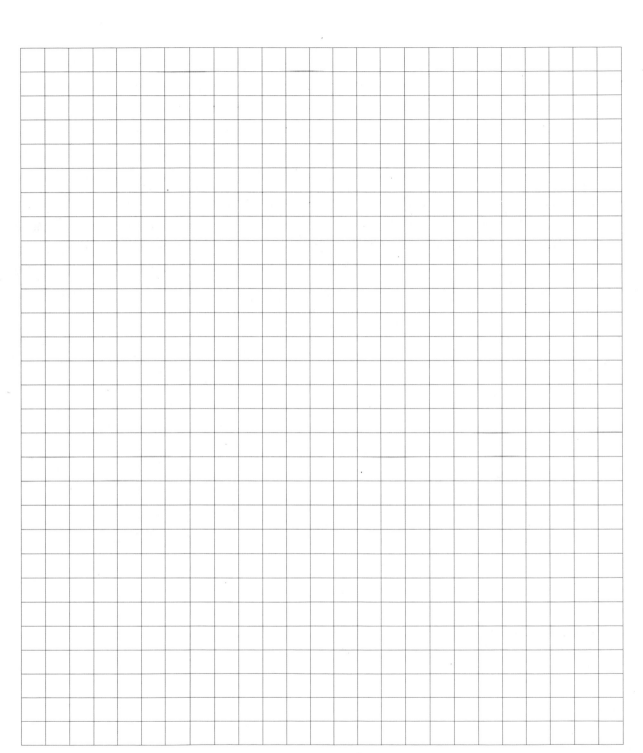

See pages 95-99 for an explanation on how to use this sheet.   1/4" measures 1'

DECK/PORCH/PATIO

DESCRIPTION OF PROJECT:

FLOOR   Dimensions: Area:

Model: Color/Style:

Manufacturer: Qty: Material: $

Purchased From: Date:

Warranty Info:

Installer/Company: Date:

Phone: Cell: Labor: $

PAINT   Dimensions: Area:

Model: Color/Style:

Manufacturer: Qty: Material: $

Purchased From: Date:

Warranty Info:

Painter/Company: Date:

Phone: Cell: Labor: $

OTHER   Dimensions: Area:

Model: Color/Style:

Manufacturer: Qty: Material: $

Purchased From: Date:

Warranty Info:

Installer/Company: Date:

Phone: Cell: Labor: $

LIGHTING/ELECTRICAL

Description	Manufacturer	Model/Style	Purchased From	Cost
				$
				$

Warranty Info:

Electrician/Company: Date:

Phone: Cell: Labor: $

DOORS/WINDOWS

Description	Dimensions	Manufacturer	Model/Style	Purchased From	Cost
Door 1					$
Door 2					$
Window 1					$
Window 2					$
Window 3					$
Window 4					$

Warranty Info:

Installer/Company: Date:

Phone: Cell: Labor: $

WINDOW/WALL COVERING

Description	Dimensions	Manufacturer	Model/Style	Purchased From	Cost
Window 1					$
Window 2					$
Window 3					$
Window 4					$
Wall 1					$
Wall 2					$

Warranty Info:

Installer/Company: Date:

Phone: Cell: Labor: $

DECORATION/FURNITURE/FIXTURES/BBQ & ACCESSORIES

Description	Manufacturer	Model/Style	Purchased From	Cost
				$
				$
				$
				$
				$

Warranty Info:

Installer/Company: Date:

Phone: Cell: Labor: $

DECK/PORCH/PATIO

GENERAL CONSTRUCTION

Description	Cost
	$
	$
	$
	$

Warranty Info:

General Contractor/Company: _____ Date: _____

Phone: _____ Cell: _____ Labor: $ _____

BUDGET ANALYSIS

Project	Budget	Actual Cost
Floor	$	$
Paint	$	$
Other:	$	$
Lighting/Electrical	$	$
Doors/Windows	$	$
Window/Wall Covering	$	$
Decoration/Furniture/Fixtures/BBQ & Accessories	$	$
General Construction	$	$
TOTAL	$	$

NOTES:

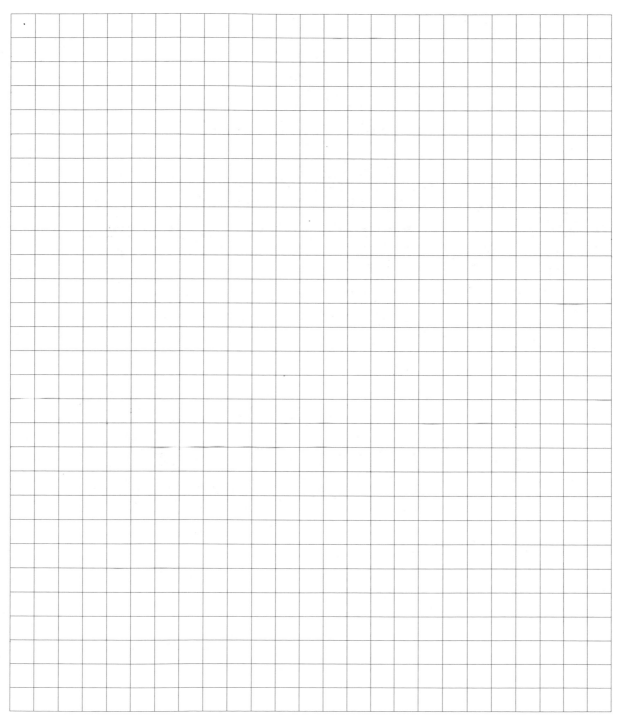

See pages 95-99 for an explanation on how to use this sheet.

1/4" measures 1'

DECK/PORCH/PATIO COVER

DESCRIPTION OF PROJECT:

PAINT   Dimensions: Area:

Model: Color/Style:

Manufacturer: Qty: Material: $

Purchased From: Date:

Warranty Info:

Painter/Company: Date:

Phone: Cell: Labor: $

LIGHTING/ELECTRICAL

Description	Manufacturer	Model/Style	Purchased From	Cost
				$

Warranty Info:

Electrician/Company: Date:

Phone: Cell: Labor: $

GENERAL CONSTRUCTION

Description	Cost
	$

Warranty Info:

General Contractor/Company: Date:

Phone: Cell: Labor: $

FIXTURES/OTHER

Description	Manufacturer	Model/Style	Purchased From	Cost
				$

Warranty Info:

Installer/Company: Date:

Phone: Cell: Labor: $

BUDGET ANALYSIS

Project	Budget	Actual Cost
Paint	$	$
Lighting/Electrical	$	$
General Construction	$	$
Fixtures/Other	$	$
TOTAL	$	$

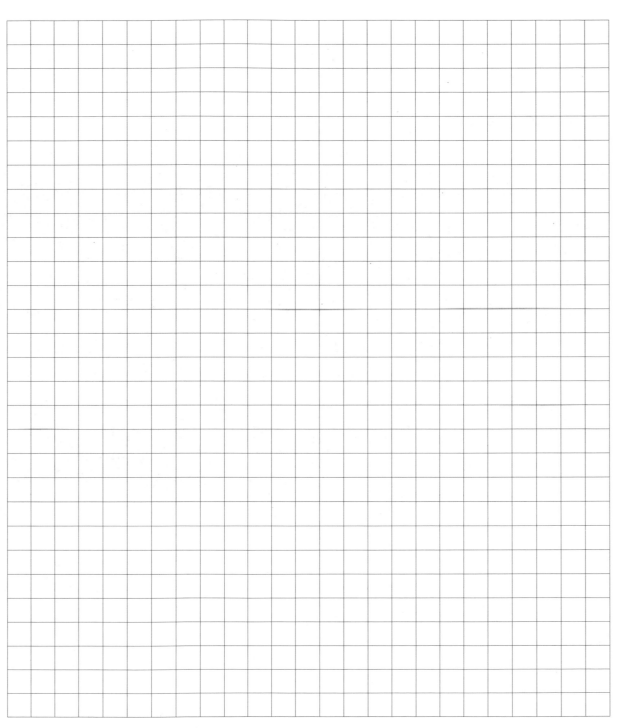

See pages 95-99 for an explanation on how to use this sheet.

1/4" measures 1'

DRIVEWAY

DESCRIPTION OF PROJECT:

_____

_____

_____

GENERAL CONSTRUCTION

Description	Cost
	$
	$
	$
	$
	$
	$
	$

Warranty Info: _____

General Contractor/Company: _____ Date: _____

Phone: _____ Cell: _____ Labor: $ _____

GENERAL SUPPLIES

Description	Manufacturer	Model/Style	Purchased From	Cost
				$
				$
				$
				$
				$
				$
				$
				$

BUDGET ANALYSIS

Project	Budget	Actual Cost
General Construction	$	$
General Supplies	$	$
TOTAL	$	$

See pages 95-99 for an explanation on how to use this sheet.   1/4" measures 1'

FENCING

DESCRIPTION OF PROJECT:

_____

_____

_____

GENERAL CONSTRUCTION

Description	Cost
	$
	$
	$
	$
	$
	$
	$

Warranty Info: _____

General Contractor/Company: _____ Date: _____

Phone: _____ Cell: _____ Labor: $ _____

GENERAL SUPPLIES

Description	Manufacturer	Model/Style	Purchased From	Cost
				$
				$
				$
				$
				$
				$
				$
				$

BUDGET ANALYSIS

Project	Budget	Actual Cost
General Construction	$	$
General Supplies	$	$
TOTAL	$	$

See pages 95-99 for an explanation on how to use this sheet.

1/4" measures 1'

GAZEBO

DESCRIPTION OF PROJECT:

FLOOR   Dimensions: Area:
Model: Color/Style:
Manufacturer: Qty: Material: $
Purchased From: Date:
Warranty Info:
Installer/Company: Date:
Phone: Cell: Labor: $

PAINT   Dimensions: Area:
Model: Color/Style:
Manufacturer: Qty: Material: $
Purchased From: Date:
Warranty Info:
Painter/Company: Date:
Phone: Cell: Labor: $

LIGHTING/ELECTRICAL

Description	Manufacturer	Model/Style	Purchased From	Cost
				$
				$

Warranty Info:
Electrician/Company: Date:
Phone: Cell: Labor: $

DECORATIONS/FURNITURE/FIXTURES

Description	Manufacturer	Model/Style	Purchased From	Cost
				$
				$

Warranty Info:
Installer/Company: Date:
Phone: Cell: Labor: $

GENERAL CONSTRUCTION

Description	Cost
	$
	$
	$
	$
	$
	$
	$

Warranty Info:

General Contractor/Company: _____ Date: _____

Phone: _____ Cell: _____ Labor: $ _____

OTHER

Description	Cost
	$
	$
	$
	$
	$
	$
	$

Warranty Info:

Installer/Company: _____ Date: _____

Phone: _____ Cell: _____ Labor: $ _____

GENERAL SUPPLIES

Description	Manufacturer	Model/Style	Purchased From	Cost
				$
				$
				$
				$
				$
				$

BUDGET ANALYSIS

Project	Budget	Actual Cost
Floor	$	$
Paint	$	$
Lighting/Electrical	$	$
Decoration/Furniture/Fixtures	$	$
General Construction	$	$
General Supplies	$	$
Other	$	$
TOTAL	$	$

NOTES:

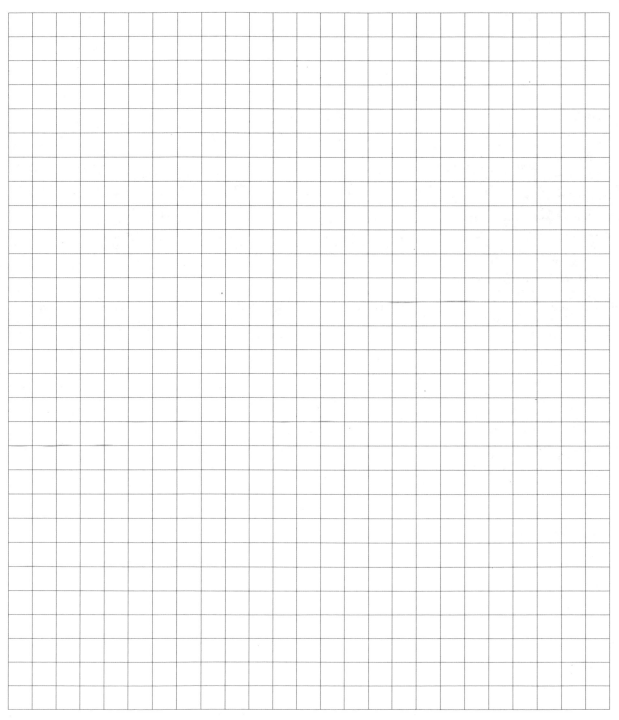

See pages 95-99 for an explanation on how to use this sheet.   1/4" measures 1'

LANDSCAPING

DESCRIPTION OF PROJECT:

WALKWAYS	Dimensions:	Area:
Model:	Color/Style:	
Manufacturer:	Qty:	Material: $
Purchased From:		Date:
Warranty Info:		
Installer/Company:		Date:
Phone:	Cell:	Labor: $

LIGHTING/ELECTRICAL

Description	Manufacturer	Model/Style	Purchased From	Cost
				$
				$
				$
				$
				$

Warranty Info:

Electrician/Company:		Date:
Phone:	Cell:	Labor: $

DECORATION/FURNITURE

Description	Manufacturer	Model/Style	Purchased From	Cost
				$
				$
				$
				$
				$

Warranty Info:

Installer/Company:		Date:
Phone:	Cell:	Labor: $

PLANTS

Description	Cost
	$
	$
	$
	$
	$
	$
	$

Care & Maintenance:

Nursery/Landscape Artist: _____ Date: _____

Phone: _____ Cell: _____ Labor: $ _____

GENERAL CONSTRUCTION

Description	Cost
	$
	$
	$
	$
	$
	$
	$

Warranty Info:

General Contractor/Company: _____ Date: _____

Phone: _____ Cell: _____ Labor: $ _____

GENERAL SUPPLIES

Description	Manufacturer	Model/Style	Purchased From	Cost
				$
				$
				$
				$
				$
				$

LANDSCAPING

BUDGET ANALYSIS

Project	Budget	Actual Cost
Walkways	$	$
Lighting/Electrical	$	$
Decorations/Furniture	$	$
Plants	$	$
General Construction	$	$
General Supplies	$	$
TOTAL	$	$

NOTES:

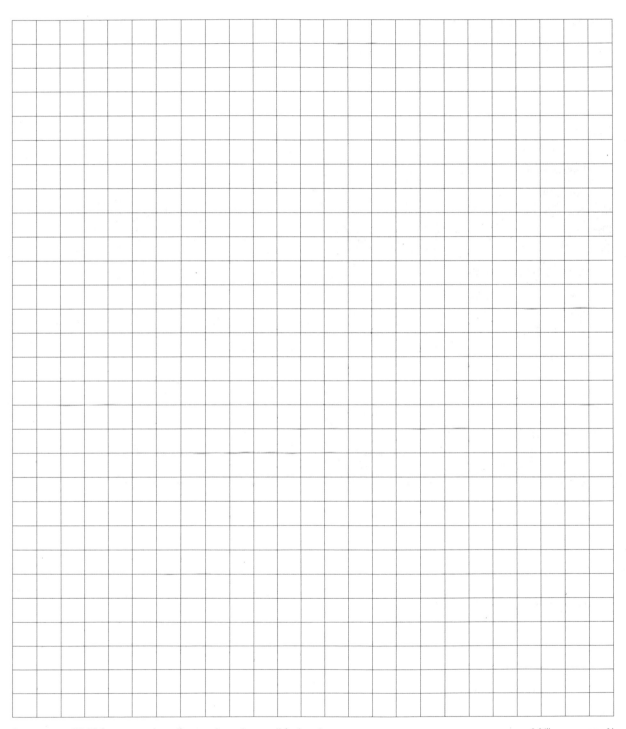

See pages 95-99 for an explanation on how to use this sheet.

1/4" measures 1'

POOL

DESCRIPTION OF PROJECT:

POOL   Dimensions: Area:

Model: Color/Style:

Manufacturer: Qty: Material: $

Purchased From: Date:

Warranty Info:

Installer/Company: Date:

Phone: Cell: Labor: $

FLOORING/WALKWAYS   Dimensions: Area:

Model: Color/Style:

Manufacturer: Qty: Material: $

Purchased From: Date:

Warranty Info:

Painter/Company: Date:

Phone: Cell: Labor: $

LIGHTING/ELECTRICAL

Description	Manufacturer	Model/Style	Purchased From	Cost
				$
				$

Warranty Info:

Electrician/Company: Date:

Phone: Cell: Labor: $

DECORATIONS/FURNITURE

Description	Manufacturer	Model/Style	Purchased From	Cost
				$
				$

Warranty Info:

Installer/Company: Date:

Phone: Cell: Labor: $

POOL SUPPLIES

Description	Cost
	$
	$
	$
	$
	$
	$
	$

Warranty Info:

Installer/Company: _____ Date: _____

Phone: _____ Cell: _____ Labor: $ _____

GENERAL CONSTRUCTION

Description	Cost
	$
	$
	$
	$
	$
	$
	$

Warranty Info:

General Contractor/Company: _____ Date: _____

Phone: _____ Cell: _____ Labor: $ _____

GENERAL SUPPLIES

Description	Manufacturer	Model/Style	Purchased From	Cost
				$
				$
				$
				$
				$
				$

POOL

BUDGET ANALYSIS

Project	Budget	Actual Cost
Pool	$	$
Flooring/Walkways	$	$
Lighting/Electrical		
Decoration/Furniture	$	$
Pool Supplies	$	$
General Construction	$	$
General Supplies	$	$
TOTAL	$	$

NOTES:

_____

_____

_____

_____

_____

_____

_____

_____

_____

_____

_____

_____

_____

_____

_____

_____

_____

_____

_____

_____

_____

_____

_____

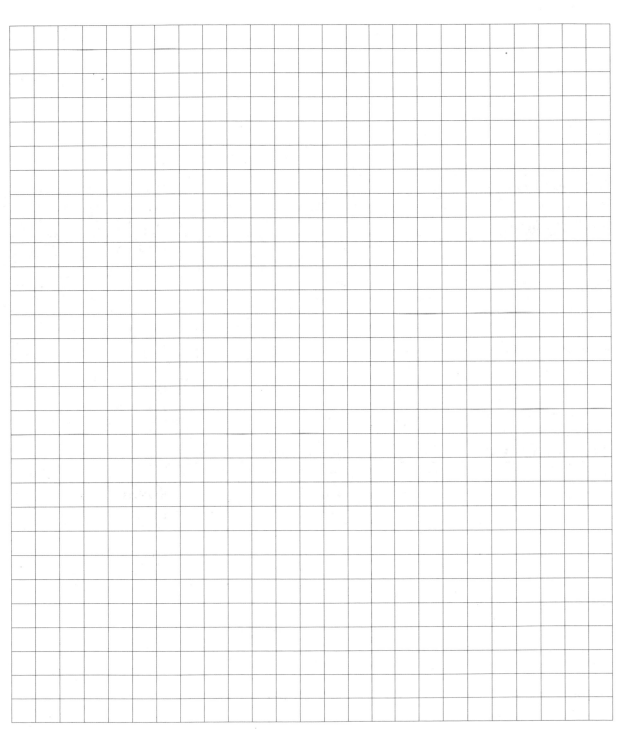

See pages 95-99 for an explanation on how to use this sheet.

1/4" measures 1'

STORAGE: GARAGE, SHEDS, ETC.

DESCRIPTION OF PROJECT:

FLOOR   Dimensions: Area:

Model: Color/Style:

Manufacturer: Qty: Material: $

Purchased From: Date:

Warranty Info:

Installer/Company: Date:

Phone: Cell: Labor: $

PAINT   Dimensions: Area:

Model: Color/Style:

Manufacturer: Qty: Material: $

Purchased From: Date:

Warranty Info:

Painter/Company: Date:

Phone: Cell: Labor: $

CABINETS/STORAGE   Dimensions:

Model: Color/Style:

Manufacturer: Qty: Material: $

Purchased From: Date:

Warranty Info:

Painter/Company: Date:

Phone: Cell: Labor: $

LIGHTING/ELECTRICAL

Description	Manufacturer	Model/Style	Purchased From	Cost
				$
				$

Warranty Info:

Electrician/Company: Date:

Phone: Cell: Labor: $

DOORS/WINDOWS

Description	Dimensions	Manufacturer	Model/Style	Purchased From	Cost
Door 1					$
Door 2					$
Window 1					$
Window 2					$
Window 3					$
Window 4					$

Warranty Info:

Installer/Company: Date:

Phone: Cell: Labor: $

WINDOW/WALL COVERING

Description	Dimensions	Manufacturer	Model/Style	Purchased From	Cost
Window 1					$
Window 2					$
Window 3					$
Window 4					$
Wall 1					$
Wall 2					$

Warranty Info:

Installer/Company: Date:

Phone: Cell: Labor: $

FIXTURES/OTHER

Description	Manufacturer	Model/Style	Purchased From	Cost
				$
				$
				$
				$
				$

Warranty Info:

Installer/Company: Date:

Phone: Cell: Labor: $

STORAGE: GARAGE, SHEDS, ETC.

GENERAL CONSTRUCTION

Description	Cost
	$
	$
	$
	$
	$
	$
	$

Warranty Info:

General Contractor/Company: _____ Date: _____

Phone: _____ Cell: _____ Labor: $ _____

BUDGET ANALYSIS

Project	Budget	Actual Cost
Floor	$	$
Paint	$	$
Cabinets/Storage	$	$
Lighting/Electrical	$	$
Doors/Windows	$	$
Window/Wall Covering	$	$
Fixtures/Other	$	$
General Construction	$	$
TOTAL	$	$

NOTES:

_____

_____

_____

_____

_____

_____

_____

See pages 95-99 for an explanation on how to use this sheet.

1/4" measures 1'

STORAGE: GARAGE, SHEDS, ETC.

NOTES:

HOME IMPROVEMENT CALENDAR

Keep yourself organized and reduce stress by tracking important dates in your renovation on the calendar pages provided. By devoting these pages entirely to your home improvement projects, you'll be able to stay streamlined and organized. It is recommended that you make note of anything that strikes you as important to remember. By documenting everything, you will find that in the event of a dispute, you will easily be able to recall any issues you may have otherwise forgotten.

Keep track of the essentials:
- Interviews with contractors
- Visits to other renovation sites
- Appointments with vendors or contractors
- Installation dates
- Expected project start and completion dates
- Home improvement shows or expos

Try to keep track of dates and events that you might not naturally think of, such as:
- Sales at local hardware, furniture and department stores
- Change order dates or other problems that occur
- Home improvement television shows pertinent to your project
- No-shows or late arrivals by contractors

Since everyone begins their renovations at different times, you will need to fill in the corresponding months in which your project will occur. We have provided 12 months of workspace, but if you anticipate your project taking longer, feel free to make photocopies of the blank pages to extend your calendar.

"What is more agreeable than one's home?"
~Marcus Tullius Cicero

MONTH: _____ **20** _____

Sunday	Monday	Tuesday	Wednesday	Thursday	Friday	Saturday

Reminders:

MONTH: _____ **20** _____

Sunday	Monday	Tuesday	Wednesday	Thursday	Friday	Saturday

Reminders: _____

MONTH: _____ **20**_____

Sunday	Monday	Tuesday	Wednesday	Thursday	Friday	Saturday

Reminders: _____

MONTH: _____ **20** _____

Sunday	Monday	Tuesday	Wednesday	Thursday	Friday	Saturday

Reminders: _____

_____

MONTH: _____ **20**____

Sunday	Monday	Tuesday	Wednesday	Thursday	Friday	Saturday

Reminders: _____

_____

MONTH: _____ **20** _____

Sunday	Monday	Tuesday	Wednesday	Thursday	Friday	Saturday

Reminders: _____

MONTH: _____ **20** _____

Sunday	Monday	Tuesday	Wednesday	Thursday	Friday	Saturday

Reminders:

MONTH: _____ **20**_____

Sunday	Monday	Tuesday	Wednesday	Thursday	Friday	Saturday

Reminders: _____

MONTH: **20**

Sunday	Monday	Tuesday	Wednesday	Thursday	Friday	Saturday

Reminders:

MONTH: _____ **20** _____

Sunday	Monday	Tuesday	Wednesday	Thursday	Friday	Saturday

Reminders: _____

MONTH: **20**

Sunday	Monday	Tuesday	Wednesday	Thursday	Friday	Saturday

Reminders:

MONTH: _____ **20** ___

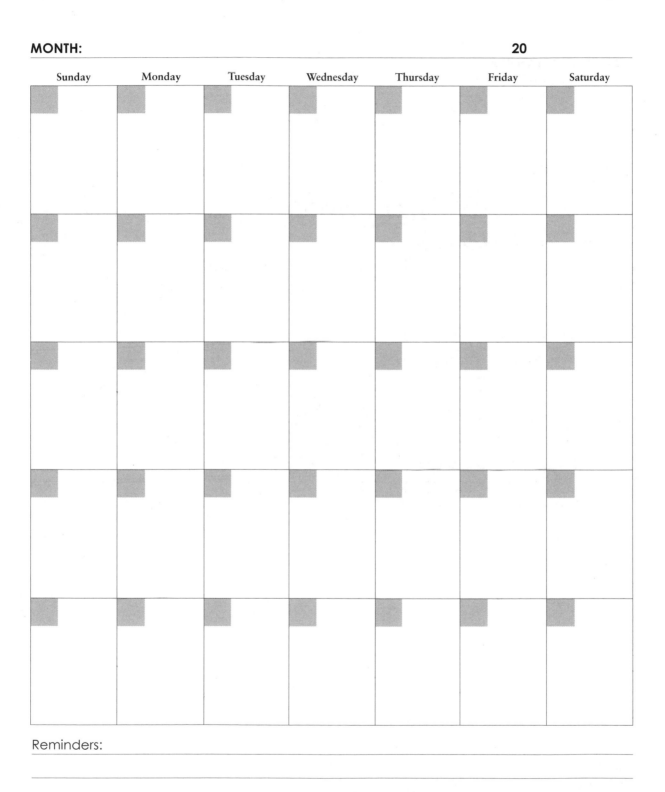

Sunday	Monday	Tuesday	Wednesday	Thursday	Friday	Saturday

Reminders: _____

DATES TO REMEMBER:

TELL US ABOUT YOUR PROJECT

We would greatly appreciate your feedback about this book. Let us know how much *The Very Best Home Improvement Guide & Document Organizer* helped you in planning and completing your project(s). We will use this information to continue improving this useful and extensive home improvement guide. Feel free to use additional sheets, if necessary.

The Very Best Home Improvement Guide & Document Organizer (helped a lot), (helped a little) in planning and completing my project. I especially liked your section on _____.

My comments about your book are: _____

_____

_____

_____

_____

The most useful part of the book was: _____

_____

_____

_____

_____

I wish your book had given me information about: _____

_____

_____

_____

_____

I would ____, would not ____ recommend this book to my friends and family.

TELL US ABOUT YOUR PROJECT

My home improvement project included: _____
_____
_____

The best thing about my project was: _____
_____
_____

The worst thing about my project was: _____
_____
_____

My advice to other people is: _____
_____
_____

This is to authorize WS Publishing Group to use my experience in any of their upcoming books. WS Publishing Group (can), (cannot) use my name when telling my story.

Name: _____
Address: _____
Home Number: _____ Work Number: _____
E-mail: _____

Signature: _____ Date: _____

Mail to WS Publishing Group:
WS Publishing Group
7290 Navajo Road
Suite 207
San Diego, California 92119

For inquiries and to review all our best-selling books:
Logon to www.WSPublishingGroup.com
E-mail info@WSPublishingGroup.com